Who Knew

Raising Kids in New York Could Be This Easy?

Who Knew

Raising Kids in New York Could Be This Easy?

FROM PLAYGROUNDS TO PRESCHOOLS, STROLLERS TO SNEAKERS, EATERIES TO EXCURSIONS...EVERYTHING A MANHATTAN PARENT WITH TOTS NEEDS TO KNOW

Heidi Arthur,
Nancy Errichetti Misshula,
& Jane Pollock

ST. MARTIN'S GRIFFIN ✖ NEW YORK

A THOMAS DUNNE BOOK.
An imprint of St. Martin's Press.

Book design by Gretchen Achilles

Library of Congress Cataloging-in-Publication Data

Arthur, Heidi.
    Who knew raising kids in New York could be this easy? : from
  playgrounds to preschools, strollers to sneakers, eateries to excur-
  sions . . . everything a Manhattan parent needs to know / by Heidi
  Arthur, Nancy Errichetti Misshula & Jane Pollock—1st ed.
        p.   cm.
    "A Thomas Dunne book."
    ISBN 0-312-18222-8
    1. Infants—Care—New York (State)—New York.   2. Toddlers—
  Care—New York (State)—New York.   3. Child rearing—New York
  (State)—New York.   I. Misshula, Nancy Errichetti.   II. Pollock,
  Jane.   III. Title.
HQ774.A77   1998
649'.122—dc21   97-35284
                                                              CIP

10 9 8 7 6 5 4 3 2

To our extraordinary children,
Alex, Ashley, Jack, and Sophie.
You've filled these pages as you have our lives.
We love you.

Acknowledgments

This book is all about collective experiences. We could not have written it without the very generous input of other New York parents. Having a child in this city is like entering a new world—a world in which everyone is excited to share information openly and give advice. As such, we are grateful to everyone who took the time to speak with us (and you know who you are). In particular, we'd like to thank Ann, Elizabeth, Victoria, Robin, Hodie, Sarah, and Amy.

We also want to thank all the agency and program directors and proprietors who let us roam around asking far too many questions.

Most importantly, we'd like to thank our husbands, Andy, Evan, and Phil, for their witty insights and their gestures of encouragement—Andy's "Who Knew" hats, Evan's chauffeuring services, and Phil's humor barometer.

Contents

Who Knew

Raising Kids in
New York
Could Be This Easy?

Introduction

We knew we were raising little New Yorkers when Sophie could hail a cab before she could walk, Alex was enrolled in more classes at four than his mom was during her freshman year, Jack insisted his friend's suburban basement, like Playspace, closed at 5 P.M., and Ashley believed that all of life's essentials could be delivered within a half hour.

Children raised in New York City are unique. They are exposed to so much so soon. Everything New York, both the good and the bad, is their reality. Its chaos, its noise, its beauty, its diversity, its intensity, its limitations, and its opportunities.

As parents, it can be overwhelming just trying to keep up with our toddlers. The list of things we need to know seems endless. Just consider some of the basics. *Preschool.* Everyone seems so anxious. Why do we believe the chatty stranger behind us in line at Gristedes is worth listening to? The process of research is daunting. *Birthday parties.* They shouldn't be such an ordeal. Does anyone really remember their second birthday party? *Childcare.* How can anyone possibly weed through all the resources out there to find the right person? You know you're in trouble when your milkman is suddenly a viable option.

As we wade through the options, we inevitably question our sanity for choosing to raise our children in New York City. Each of us has had our fair share of eye-rolling, wishing-we-lived-somewhere-else, and desperately-in-need-of-help days.

Heidi: *I had my first, Alex, before any of my friends had children. I quickly became the master of winging it. Working full-time, having an infant, and living in a barely one bedroom apartment certainly had the makings for a soon-to-be suburban family. Without friends as resources, it was pretty hard to figure it all out. I got my first nanny from my doorman, whom I barely knew, but I felt that the connection to my building was the fewest concrete degrees of separation I was going to find. From about six months to two years, I seemed to have things under control. Then along came the whole preschool thing—at the time, please remember, no one I knew had a clue (or kids), so neither did I. I was at a summer outing for my husband's office when I overheard a conversation among four older moms. It was something like, "Oh, yes, we did get in there; with your connections, I can't believe you were only wait-listed." I looked around thinking I would see a bunch of college bound kids. But, much to my surprise, the offspring in question were all in the kiddy pool with water wings. Oops, I had no idea that you actually had to apply to preschool so soon. Now, six years later with a second child in preschool, I'm the one that people ask for help. Take Jane, for instance. We met at work. Once she had Jack, we were in each other's offices all the time. It was fun to trade anecdotes. We became incredibly skilled at turning a funny story about the children into a discussion on how to solve a client dispute when anyone entered the room. Nancy and I have been friends forever. We have known each other in such different phases of life that we can't help but giggle every once in a while about the fact that some human beings actually call us "Mommy." We have counted on each other through lots of things; parenthood is no exception.*

Jane: *I really love New York. I grew up in the suburbs of Boston, hate to drive, love ethnic food, and have no interest in lawn care. My husband and I had lots of pre-family time here. We ate brunch as late as we wanted to, went to museums all the time, lived down the street from CBGBs, and never considered the need for a good playground nearby. When I first got pregnant, I was convinced that my life wouldn't change all that much. I envisioned doing much of the same with a baby in tow. For the first few months after Jack was born, I really didn't like New York. Nothing* was the same. Even the simplest things seemed impossible. Like going somewhere, for instance. Just to get out of the apartment building, I had to hold the door open with my left foot, kick the diaper bag out on to the sidewalk with my right, clench my keys in my mouth, and propel the carriage through the doorway before it slammed shut. Why did I buy such a big stroller? OK, so one day I was finally out the door at six (A.M., that is), and all I wanted to do was take my colicky baby for a walk on the cobble stones, hoping it would soothe him. I grabbed a cup of coffee, pushed the stroller, and spilled it all over the only shirt I had that wasn't prestained by Jack. Not quite my fantasy of maternity leave. I called my husband at his office. He was pleasantly sympathetic, but empathy would have gone a lot further. I wish someone had told me about the ten other mothers who met at a nearby parenting center to lament and laugh about it all. Knowing how hard it can be to be a brand new mom, particularly in New York, I'm always the first to offer any tidbits that will help. Things have certainly changed, but I can honestly say that I love New York again. Raising a child here has actually opened up a whole new city for me. While I can't have brunch wherever, whenever, I can go to a lot of the same places, though it's usually for an early dinner. We still enjoy museums, spending more time at the Arms & Armor exhibit at the Met than at a photography exhibit at MOMA. I now know what a lifesaver playgrounds can be, and Jack and I can detect them a mile away. Life's definitely different. But different, in this case, is clearly better.

Nancy: I was quite sure by my early thirties that I had it all pretty much figured out. I knew enough about myself to find my perfect match in Evan (OK, maybe a little luck was involved). I was a litigator practicing with a large law firm in the city. Along the way, I had the opportunity to develop some of my natural tendencies. I was a champion listmaker. The longer the list, the more challenging to complete it in the least amount of time. My apartment, my office, and my briefcase were super-organized. I even thought out the work/family issue before getting pregnant and decided to start a consulting service for New York parents (with Maria, a litigation colleague). We wanted to ease the time crunch for working parents by helping them identify infant/toddler, pre-

school, and after-school programs for their children. I wanted something meaningful to do that would also allow me the time to be a mom. And I figured if the business didn't work out, I would have a tremendous amount of information with which to raise my children in the city. Then, along came the light of my life—Sophie Ann. And as the saying goes, nothing was ever the same again. I still make lists except now they're never completed because they include such tasks as (1) call Jane to find a restaurant with decent food that won't mind Sophie's habit of flinging hers; (2) call Heidi to confirm that Alex and Ashley loved Diller-Quaile; and (3) call anybody I can think of to see if they know of a nanny who is looking for a job. Speaking of nannies, there was nothing more humbling, especially for someone who has made a career of asking questions, than sitting across from the first nanny I ever interviewed and trying to ask questions that were simultaneously piercing, legal, and welcoming. After all, what is a tactful way of finding out whether she is post-pubescent or wanted in forty-nine states? Whew! Despite all the factual research I had done, nothing made me feel as good about my choices for Sophie as hearing the inside skinny from seasoned New York moms like my good friends Heidi and Jane. I could always count on the two of them for sage advice, funny war stories, and great tips. For a new parent living in a big city that presents lots of choices, there is no substitute for a good friend with children a little older than your precious one—until now.

In some ways our experiences in New York City have been very different. But we certainly have a lot of common ground. We all know that the more we share with one another and with our other friends, the better our parenting will be. We also share a belief that we are lucky to be bringing up our children here.

Raising children in New York City can be amazing. There are millions of magical moments just waiting to happen here. Even the most pedestrian events can be full of wonder for your child. Whether it's giving your child pennies to throw in the wishing pool at the Met, teaching her to ride a bike on Literary Walk, or leaving your office to meet him for lunch at the zoo in Central Park, New York can be a wonderful place for parents of young children. That is, with a little help from us.

Who Knew Raising Kids in New York Could Be This Easy? may well end up being your best friend. It will hold your hand as you navigate through New York City with tots. *Who Knew* is chock full of relevant information. It covers all of parents' day-to-day issues from the most pressing (*who will care for my child when I can't?*) to the more mundane (*where can I get a good kiddy haircut without making my own hair stand on end?*).

Who Knew is not intended to inundate you with facts or to serve as a guidebook for out-of-towners. Rather, it is designed to share firsthand, frank, and essential information for people who live here. In fact, *Who Knew* was written by people who do know—three parents of New York City tots. Among us, we've gone through it all. We've dealt with childcare, applied to programs and preschools, thrown birthday parties, shopped, dined, babyproofed, bought infant Tylenol at 2 A.M., and left skid marks in search of greener pastures just for the afternoon.

In writing this book, we have met a lot of wonderful parents who were eager to share their information with us. It seems that almost everyone is passionate about what they have experienced in New York City with their children. This book reflects not only our own experiences, but also those of other parents.

To continue this joint effort, we'd love to include your thoughts in future editions. So please send information on your own great finds to *Who Knew* c/o St. Martin's Press, 175 Fifth Avenue, New York, New York 10010 or by e-mail to whoknew@stmartins.com.

Who Knew will be the kind of book you find yourself reaching for over and over—we've actually been referring to the drafts of this book ourselves. Our hope is that *Who Knew* will be a security blanket for the big issues, an eye opener to a city of new possibilities for family fun, and the most insightful phone book you've ever picked up on the smaller day-to-day questions. (And remember, the city changes as quickly as your child, so be sure to call before you venture out.) We hope you'll stuff it into your diaper bag, carry it in your briefcase, and leave a second copy near the phone.

CHAPTER 1

It's 8:00 A.M.: Do You Know Where Your Babysitter Is?

CHILDCARE

Finding the right childcare situation is probably the most important and the most traumatic decision any parent can make. The magnitude of this issue is the same whether you are away all week for ten hours a day or just for a few hours on a Saturday night.

In New York City, this decision can prompt lots of nail biting. After all, you are looking for a person to care for your child in one of the biggest cities in the world. However, with the right information and good use of the city's resources available you can achieve peace of mind. This city can be a childcare mecca once you've done your homework, participated in many interviews, tossed and turned, and finally made a decision.

We cover three childcare situations: at-home childcare, all-day childcare programs, and temporary/last minute care.

At-Home Childcare

At-home childcare can offer maximum flexibility for those with ever-changing schedules. Options include live-in/out nannies and au pairs. It can be comforting to know that someone is there to accommodate those unavoidable late afternoon meetings and never-ending subway delays. On the downside, at-home care can be very costly ($300/week at a minimum), and one can become hostage to a baby-sitter unless a back-up plan is in place.

We have listed several agencies to help you find the right child-care situation. Of course, there are many others. If you choose to use an agency, be sure to get their license number and check on them with the Department of Consumer Affairs (487-4444). Also, consider the following:

➡ Fee

➡ Average salary of nanny

➡ Guarantee of satisfaction

➡ Background checks/references provided

➡ Education/experience of applicants (are there minimum standards?)

➡ Child CPR certification (will they pay for instruction for those not certified?)

Having said all this, you don't necessarily have to use a service to find the right help. Not only do the services charge a fee, but they are not always foolproof (after all, your decision is their paycheck). Word of mouth can be an invaluable tool in the search for the right caregiver, so explore the following:

➡ Friends

➡ Other nannies you know and like

➡ Doorman/superintendent

➡ Pediatrician

➡ Coworkers

➡ Temple/church

➡ *Irish Echo* (where few are Irish) and *The New York Times*

➡ Job posting boards at program facilities and schools

➡ You, too, can post a job description at local universities

All Home Services Agency
2121 Broadway
799-9360
Contact: Nedra Kleinman

Calling Nedra is almost like calling your own mother for advice—she's very warm and frank. She wants everybody to be happy: both families and nannies. The fee, six weeks of a nanny's salary for live-in and four weeks for live-out positions, is not due until all involved are feeling like the situation is a good one. If you decide within ninety-days that you are not satisfied, they guarantee a replacement. The average weekly salary ranges from $350.00 to $700.00 depending on the nanny's education level and references—which may be star studded.

Mom's Services Inc.
1556 Third Avenue
410-6700
Contact: Rebecca Coren

Unlike some others, this agency has a straight fee of $1800. The average salary ranges from $350.00 to $450.00 on the books. All prospective nannies have agency-verified green cards and are not United States citizens. Most of these nannies not only will cook and care for your children but also will do light housekeeping. The guarantee here is good: for the first thirty days, ninety percent of the fee is refundable or they will replace the nanny. After sixty days, they will replace the nanny free of charge. Once the nanny is placed, she is obligated to pay for a CPR class for herself.

Nannies of Nebraska
125 South Fourth Street
P.O. Box 2202
Norfolk, Nebraska 68702
402-379-2444
Contact: Candi Wingate

A huge time-saver for parents on the prowl for a nanny, this agency conducts extensive prescreening of nannies and clearly understands employers' needs and expectations— no surprises here on either end. The nannies come from the Midwest and range in age from nineteen on up. They are required to have spent at least one year living away from home (thus avoiding lots of homesick tears behind closed doors). Salaries range from $225 to $500 per week. Guarantees are like insurance policies here, the more you pay the more you get. For example, the lowest fee of $1750 buys you a 50% refund of the fee after thirty days, and a replacement for up to sixty days.

New York Nanny Center
31 South Bayles Avenue
Port Washington, NY 11050
516-767-5136
Contact: Carol Solomon

If you want a camp counselor type, call here. The live-in nannies are young (eighteen to twenty-five) and tend to be from the Midwest and Northwest. The live-out nannies are from the New York area and tend to be college students. The agency carefully screens the nannies to ensure that they are emotionally and physically healthy and have great, relevant experience. In fact, the agency travels to meet each nanny in her hometown. The nannies are given sixteen essay questions and must provide three recent references. The agency also uses a private investigator to do a criminal and motor vehicle check. The fee is $1800 (live-in) or four weeks of your nanny's salary (live-out.) You pay round trip airfare for your nanny based on her commitment to stay for one year. If she doesn't stay, then she is responsible.

Robin Kellner Agency
221 West 57th Street
247-4141
Contact: Robin Kellner

Robin Kellner founded this agency ten years ago as a new parent. She handpicks prospective nannies as if she were hiring them to care for her own children. The fee is four weeks of the nanny's salary payable at the end of the first month ($1750 minimum for live-out and ten percent of annual gross salary for live-in). The average salary is $350 per week. Robin guarantees a free replacement within sixty days or a prorated refund equal to the agency fee less twenty percent of your nanny's total earnings.

AU PAIR AGENCIES

An au pair can be a surprisingly affordable (less than $200 a week) way to provide your family with live-in childcare. Most au pairs are young European women (usually eighteen to twenty-four) who want to experience a new culture in exchange for providing childcare. A few things to consider:

➡ Hours are restricted—usually to a maximum of forty-five per week

➡ Most are here for only one year

➡ They may not be permitted to stay alone overnight with the children

➡ They may not be suitable for newborns

➡ They have strict vacation guidelines which may not fit your needs

➡ They may be tall, skinny, and blonde

Most agencies can provide summer au pairs that will stay with your family for ten weeks—what a great way to get an extra set of hands at the beach. Au pairs usually command a minimum of $45 to $50 per week in the summer. But don't be too impressed—the application and program fee can run up to $1100. Of course, simple math will still show significant cost savings over traditional live-in/out childcare.

Au Pair in America
102 Greenwich Avenue
Greenwich, CT 06830
800-928-7247

InterExchange Au Pair
161 6th Avenue
924-0446

EF Au Pair
One Memorial Drive
Cambridge, MA 02142
800-333-6056

DOUBLE CHECKING

Once you've chosen a caregiver, you may still feel a bit queasy. We have listed some surveillance services that give you the power to be both a fly on the wall and a background check agency, so you don't have to play private eye.

Child Visual Guard, Inc.
744-3796

For some, seeing is believing. Child Visual Guard will rent you a concealed video surveillance system so you can spy on your caregiver interacting with your child. They will install the equipment and pick it up when you are through. A one-day peek might be enough for you, but there is a two-day minimum.

Kid-View, Inc.
516-869-6998

Billing themselves as mind easers, this company has state-of-the-art hidden video surveillance systems. Be prepared for the consequences, as they claim that sixty-five percent of those parents who use the service end up firing the caregiver.

The ChildCare Registry
800-CCR-0033

If your childcare provider has nothing to hide, she won't mind signing a release allowing ChildCare Registry to check her history and credentials. For $140, the company verifies her identity, criminal and driving records, employment history, references, and educational claims. While you're at it, it might be fun to do the same for your spouse.

All-Day Childcare Programs

The term *daycare* has become somewhat of a misnomer and carries with it certain misconceptions. The conventional wisdom is that daycare is nothing more than glorified baby-sitting, a cheaper alternative to in-home childcare, or a short-term situation until the child is of preschool age. However, a visit around Manhattan to the wonderful programs available demonstrates that the daycare paradigm has certainly changed. (And hey, this is not new news ... some of these programs have been around for over fifteen years.)

The reality of these programs is that they offer all-day childcare in conjunction with early childhood education for infants and toddlers. Whether its bottles or meals, hugs or high fives, diaper changes or trips to the potty, naps or just rest, their emotional and physical needs are amply met. From an educational standpoint, the programs offer developmentally appropriate curricula including field trips, specialty classes (e.g., foreign language, music, movement), and indoor or outdoor physical activities.

For many New Yorkers, these programs provide a welcome alternative to at-home childcare or traditional preschool. After talking to many parents and program directors, we came up with a list of advantages:

➡ **Commuting parents.** Uptown to downtown or vice versa, it's comforting to be within a few minutes of your baby. We saw many suited moms and dads pop in for a cuddle and a kiss during the day.

➡ **Traditional preschool limitations.** Many preschools do not accept children until they are almost three; they often do not provide a long enough day to fit parents' needs. Some parents are so happy with their all-day program that they keep their children in through pre-K despite the wealth of great preschools in their neighborhoods.

➡ **Sense of community.** It takes the isolation out of parenting an infant. With so many people in the same boat there are many opportunities for positive parental reinforcement and lasting relationships. It's nice for the parent rather than the caregiver to be the center of new social relationships.

➡ **You're late, it's not.** Perfect for parents with pressing morning schedules.

➡ **Comfort in numbers.** Lots of qualified people are around to handle any emergency situation.

➡ **You always know where your child is.** It can be nerve-wracking to phone home during your child's supposed nap time, only to find no one at home.

➡ **Built-in playmates.** A lot of other children are there providing plenty of opportunity to socialize and eliminating the need for the infamous play date calendar.

When checking out a program bear in mind the following:

➡ **Hours.** Are they flexible, extended—early or late?

➡ **Holiday schedules.** Will they be open?

➡ **Credentials.** Are they national/state/city accredited?

➡ **Adult-child ratio.** It's comforting to see one exceeding the minimum standards.

➡ **Degrees/Certification** (of center's directors, teachers, and aides).

➡ **Program offerings**

➡ **Parent conferences**

➡ **Sick children.** What is their policy?

➡ **Outdoor play facilities.** Are there any? Are parks nearby and how are the children transported to them?

➡ **Turnover of personnel**

➡ **Meals.** Do you need to provide them for your child?

➡ **Nap schedules.** While your child may be consistent, the program may not be.

All this does not come cheap. Fees range from approximately $850 to $1000 per month and some programs require a school year commitment. Call each program for tuition details.

Children's All Day School and Pre Nursery
109 East 60th Street
752-4566
Director: Mrs. Hewitt
Ages: six months through pre-K

Housed in a brownstone, this school offers a warm and charming environment in which infants and toddlers feel right at home. Aside from the reputable program and teachers who never leave, this school boasts a wonderful, large redwood-decked play yard, rare in New York City. The yard includes a real tree house, a separate young toddler play area, a sandbox, and lots of other fun stuff. The infant room has a big window onto this play world, full of quality visual stimulation. Each classroom has a loft area and all are bright, sunny, and art-filled. Also noteworthy is Harvey, the music teacher, who we are told has quite a loyal following. Open daily from 8:00 A.M. to 6:00 P.M., they offer lots of flexibility in scheduling.

Buckle My Shoe Learning Center
40 Worth Street
374-1489
230 West 13th Street
807-0518
Director: Linda Ensko, M. Ed.
Ages: three months (Worth Street only) through pre-K

A hyper-stimulated environment housed in an 8,000-square-foot space, this program offers a wide variety of creative educational and physical activities. It covers everything from karate to French to woodworking to gardening to good old-fashioned fun. This cavernous space can get quite noisy, but don't worry—the babies have a separate nap room. Although the program doesn't have outdoor space, they've more than made up for it with an indoor gym complete with swings and with trips to nearby parks. A look around revealed lots of creative art and science projects in the works. The 13th Street location is physically quite different as it is housed in a small brownstone and starts at age two. Both locations are open from 8:00 A.M. to 6:00 P.M. and have flexible scheduling options.

University Early Childhood Learning Center
45 University Place
228-5437
Director: Audrey Golden
Ages: twenty-two months through pre-K

Although physically smaller than others, this place has a
creative, lofty feel to it. The ceilings are high, the rooms are
bright, and they've built an indoor tree house for kids only.
The staff is young and energetic and they encourage the
kids to color outside the lines. In fact, on one day, the children were actually allowed to paint the walls themselves.
The walls are covered with lots of kiddy masterpieces. Of
special note, there's a separate computer room with six
computers and lots of fun software. There is no outdoor
space attached, but they do like to take the kids outside in
nearby Washington Square Park. For parents in a bind, they
also have a drop-off program called Flights of Fancy, where
you can call early in the morning to drop off a child for any
or all hours from 8:00 A.M. to 6:00 P.M.

Your Kids, Our Kids
30 West 15th Street
675-6226
Director: Debra Coppolino
Ages: three months through pre-K

Perfect for those who need to get an early start, the facility
opens at 7:30 A.M. The physical space is large, clean, and
fairly new (established 1992) with a family-friendly feel.
They try to make your life as easy as possible recognizing
how hectic mornings can be. All you have to do is bring
your child. They provide breakfast, lunch, and an afternoon
snack for toddlers, and bottles (but not formula), diapers,
baby food, bedding, and cereal for infants. The program is
developmentally appropriate and, with no attached outdoor
space, the children visit Union Square Park with its familiar
Greenmarket.

Battery Park City Day Nursery
215 South End Avenue
945-0088
Directors: Denise Cordivano and Karen Klomp
Ages: one year through pre-K

This center provides a secure, nurturing, and creative environment where children feel quite at home learning and playing. Just take a look around. This program is housed in an apartment building (practically taking over the first floor), and each cheerful classroom feels like a little home with its own kitchen and bathroom (great for cooking projects or potty training). The outdoor space is accessible from most rooms and has lots of age appropriate equipment and a huge playhouse. The staff is especially warm and caring. Our naptime visit showed lots of back rubbing and soft singing. This school prides itself on a strong sense of community with families enjoying events such as the annual spring barbecue. Open from 8:00 A.M. to 6:00 P.M.

Trinity Parish Preschool and Nursery
74 Trinity Place
602-0829
Director: Nadine Geyer
Ages: six months through pre-K

At Trinity's brand spankin' new digs, a wall of tropical fish and a squawking parrot greeted us with much enthusiasm. Speaking of enthusiasm, this program has become so popular that even embryonic enrollment is encouraged (a place on the waitlist is $250). Located in the heart of the financial district, it allows many parents to commute with their children from other parts of the city. All of the classrooms are cheerful and filled with creativity. The staff is highly experienced and turnover is low. The infant rooms are almost like having a second nursery for your baby, well equipped with all the latest and greatest stuff. The environment is warm and loving. When we were there, the children were happily bouncing to "If you're happy and you know it . . ." and a visiting dad was happily bouncing too. Although they have use of the church yard, they visit local playgrounds. They also have a large indoor gymnasium. Open from 8:00 A.M. to 6:00 P.M.

Temporary/Last Minute Care

Whether you choose at-home childcare or a daycare center, there inevitably comes a day when everything unravels. Either your nanny calls in sick or your child has a raging fever and obviously can't go to daycare. Of course, this is the day that you have a critical don't-show-up-and-you're-fired kind of meeting. You need some help. These places can be lifesavers on very short notice.

Babysitters' Guild
60 E. 42nd Street, Suite 912
682-0227

Speak to Heidi or Louis, who do all the booking. This service is well known and used by affluent out-of-towners (staying in places like The Carlyle, The Mark, The Stanhope.) Their sitters are exceedingly punctual and can be procured on very short notice (if you like someone, you can even request them again). They require a four-hour minimum and they are not cheap—$14.50 per hour plus $4.50 for transportation before midnight and $7.00 after midnight.

Pinch Sitters
799 Broadway, Suite 204
260-6005

Their motto, "child care for your unpredictable life," couldn't ring more true. Pinch Sitters specialize in one thing and one thing only, and they're great at it. Unlike some others, they open at 7:00 A.M. and can generally find someone for you even at the last minute. They feature college-educated or professional women who have experience with children as well as experience in getting somewhere on time. They charge $10.00 an hour, and if you're out after 9:00 P.M., you're responsible for the sitter's transportation home.

CHAPTER 2

Stuff, Stuff, and More Stuff

PARAPHERNALIA

Just contemplating how to accessorize a child can be a mind-boggling experience, even for the most competent of parents. There are so many things that need to be purchased and so many places from which to choose. And for parents of New York tots, decisions become more complicated; they are all about space—or the lack thereof. Parents are no longer the kings of their castles—they're merely squeezed-out subjects in the child's kingdom.

Obvious space limitations combined with the array of exciting things to do right outside the door make finding the best mode of transportation for your baby something to take seriously. You'll also find yourself wondering what to do with all the stuff that your child has outgrown (both big and small) as you'll need to make room for even more stuff. So, in addition to suggesting stuff you'll need, places to buy stuff, and stuff to think about for transporting baby, we've also suggested some dumping grounds for used stuff.

Inside Stuff

The following are big things to consider for your little New Yorker:

➡ **Bassinet.** Takes up a lot less room than a crib for the first three months.

➡ **Swing.** While it is not a space saver, it can be a lifesaver.

➡ **Bouncy seat.** Compact, travels well, multi-purpose.

➡ **Highchair on wheels.** After all, you eat just about anywhere in an apartment.

➡ **Sassy seat.** Travels well and takes up less space than a high chair.

➡ **Dresser with changing table on top.** Goes without saying.

➡ **Portable crib.** Great for visits to the in-laws and weekend trips, and stores easily.

➡ **Travel & trundle bed.** Good for toddlers who are out of the crib.

➡ **Play mat.** Soft padding for wood floors.

➡ **Car seat.** Borrow it; unlike suburban friends, you won't use it much.

➡ **Bath tub ring or sponge insert.** Great for baths in the kitchen sink.

➡ **Potty seat.** Yes, they all eventually get trained (consider a portable one).

➡ **Bike seat.** Doesn't take up more room than your bike already does.

➡ **Child safety harness.** Great for restraining in that wild taxi ride.

➡ **Diaper genie.** Smells travel fast in small places.

Baby Transportation

Buying a stroller for New York warrants as much thought and deliberation as buying a car for the suburbs. After all, it will be your child's most frequent mode of transportation. Before becoming dead set on the super deluxe oversized model, remember that you live in New York City and do the following:

➡ Do a run-through of your most frequented neighborhood stores to check aisle width, entrance ways, sharp turns.

➡ Simulate hailing and loading a taxi—place a doll in one arm (representing baby) and an overstuffed diaper bag over one shoulder; then collapse the stroller, assuming no help from the driver or numerous passersby.

➡ Look at the stroller's hang space and underneath storage for diaper bags and shopping bags.

➡ Think about how you will clean the seat and hood (in this city you'll want to) as some are not removable.

➡ Consider whether or not your place of purchase will service your stroller (check under the canopy and rotate the wheels).

Another popular mode of baby transportation is the soft pack (Snuglies, Baby Bjorns). This device allows you to strap on the baby while you shop, walk, work, clean, or travel stroller-free. An added bonus, especially during those postpartum summer months, is the drape effect. No one will be able to see, feel, or contemplate the size of your supposedly deflated belly behind this device.

No matter how you travel, consider these amenities for your baby and yourself:

➡ **Cup holder for stroller.** It's hard to push and not spill (usually on you).

➡ **Ice pack for bottle.** Just remember how you feel about warm Diet Coke.

➡ **Backpack diaper bag.** The more free hands, the better.

- → **Juice box holder.** The spill theory applies here.

- → **Toy bar for stroller.** A little amusement goes a long way.

- → **Rain cover for stroller.** Yes, they *can* breathe in these plastic bubbles.

- → **Stroller blanket/bunting.** Brr . . . goes without saying.

- → **Snack pack.** Great for the ever-popular Cheerios fix.

- → **Netted stroller bag.** Ugly, but oh-so-functional.

STORES

Albees Baby Carriage Company, Inc.
715 Amsterdam Avenue at 95th Street
662-5740, 8902

Albees provides one stop shopping to completely accessorize a newborn. From bottles to strollers, Albees has it all. The prices are reasonable and the service is great (the employee-owners give good advice and don't try to push things you don't need). It's really not a place to come to make up your "things I want to buy" list. Also, while you may not, Albees delivers on time and will assemble all equipment (just call when you need it). The stroller selection is broad, but test drive elsewhere, as space is limited. Try to avoid the crowds on Saturday afternoons as you can wait up to a half hour for help with a chorus of unhappy babies to soothe your nerves.

Plain Jane Inc.
525 Amsterdam Avenue between 85th and 86th Streets
595-6916

A visit to Plain Jane is great for those who are tired of the same old, plain old. Their accessories and furniture are truly beautiful, unique, and reasonably priced (everything is relative). Notable examples are the bumper set made of chenille, one-of-a-kind quilts, made-to-order duvets, antique-like beds, and bookshelves with decoupage. This is one of the few stores that gives equal preference to boys. The bunk bed with built-in bookshelves and the western themed linens break ground in designs for boys. They also have a small selection of children's clothing and shoes.

Ben's for Kids
1380 Third Avenue between 78th and 79th Streets
794-2330

This well-organized, well-stocked store is a great place for one-stop, top-of-the-line shopping at top prices. You can basically furnish your child's room, find cute bedding, test drive a stroller, buy bottles and layette items, sling on some diaper bags, and daydream about potty training without ever leaving the store. The atmosphere is relaxed and crowds are not a big issue here.

Portico Kids
1167 Madison Avenue at 86th Street
717-1963

Portico Kids is the crème de la crème for fine baby furniture. Don't come here for strollers or bottles (they don't sell them) but if you're looking for beautiful bedding and furniture, it cannot be beat. From incredible cotton fabrics to sophisticated wrought-iron cradles (future heirlooms), Portico Kids is for the baby with many silver spoons. If your baby is due in the spring or if you shop in advance, Portico has a great winter sale.

Schneider's Baby Carriages
20 Avenue A at Second Street
228-3540

Schneider's offers a complete range of baby equipment including strollers, carriages, cribs, bumper sets, and bedding. Their selection of smaller items (bottles, pacifiers, pajamas) is more limited. They offer most high-end stroller brands but tend to push the Maclaren even if you'd rather push a Peg Perego. For uptowners, it can be a fun escapade to Alphabet City.

Baby Palace
1410 Lexington Avenue between 92nd and 93rd
Streets
426-4544

Conveniently located near the 92nd Street Y, Baby Palace is perfect for one-stop shopping and comfortable browsing. Filled with great developmental toys, lots of accessories, and big items such as strollers, furniture, and car seats, it's a good place to walk around and pick up ideas for things you'll need. The salespeople are helpful and leave you alone. Even more helpful are some of the shoppers who are eager and willing to give advice on items and help you with decisions. The prices are competitive with most places.

Burlington Coat Factory Baby Depot
116 West 23rd Street at Sixth Avenue
229-2247

High above the Burlington Coat Factory, The Baby Depot is a great place for functional accessories at a good discount. Necessities such as bottles, safety devices, and Diaper Genie refills are sold at roughly 30% less than retail. They also carry a vast selection of big items like strollers (anything from Emmeljunga to Graco), car seats, high chairs, exersaucers, cribs/dressers (mostly Child craft and Simmons), bedding/bumper sets, and booster seats. It's a good place to shop with toddlers as they have a small reading area complete with table and chairs for those weary little feet. The tot rest area is, however, right next to the escalator. (Your nerves may need a rest.)

Little Folks
123 East 23rd Street between Park and Lexington
Avenues
982-9669

This is not the place to go to feel all warm and fuzzy about pending parenthood. Instead, it's the place to go to feel all warm and fuzzy about your wallet. The store is a little cluttered and musty, but the selection of strollers, car seats, and accessories is quite extensive. The prices seemed to be somewhat lower than other places with a little room to go even lower. The salespeople are friendly, upfront, and demonstrative. We can tell you firsthand that the Combi umbrella stroller will not give in to 200 pounds of baby—yes, the salesman sat on it to prove its durability.

Kid's Supply Co.
1325 Madison Avenue between 93rd and 94th
Streets
426-1200

Yes, there is life beyond the crib, and Kid's Supply Co. makes the transition something you can look forward to (aesthetically speaking, that is). They have a beautiful selection of new and antique, trundle and bunk beds that are sure to entice your tot into sleeping in her *own* bed. You will, however, have to shop elsewhere for the Barney sheets that are the *real* treat for the bed bound toddler. Try not to promise them until you have already checked out the linens, quilts, and pillows at Kid's Supply Co.

Iddy Biddy Bedding Company
Jill Goret
201-597-9334

Even expectant moms confined to iddy biddy bed rest can
shop for exquisite custom children's bedding (from crib to
big bed). If you can't make the trek to New Jersey, owner
Jill Goret will make a house call (and she may well have a
better bedside manner than most obstetricians). She carries
twenty different lines of one-of-a-kind bedding and offers
unique items such a chenille bumper sets and vintage antique quilts. All this at a twenty percent discount is sure to
make most parents rest easy.

Dumping Grounds

Start with your pregnant friend. Be the first to offer her your
stuff. But don't stop there. Also be the first to offer your stuff to
your friend who is due six months after your first friend (remember, you do not want your super-deluxe swing dropped back off
at your building eight months after you thought you'd never see it
again). With proper orchestration and a good supply of pregnant
friends, most of your stuff will never show up again, unless you
want it.

It feels good to give; however, it also feels good to recoup some
of the money you have dished out for all this stuff. Resale stores
are a good option for those who have taken good care of equipment
and used bibs religiously.

Good-Byes Children's Resale Store for Clothing
& Toys
230 East 78th Street between Second and
Third Avenues
794-2301

Clean your closets and make an appointment at Good-
Byes. This store will take clothes, equipment, and toys
(no stuffed animals, dolls, or games) and sell them at

fifty percent of their original value. You, in turn, get forty percent of the resale price for clothes and toys and fifty percent for equipment. They are, however, selective in what they'll take. For example, only Peg Perego and Maclaren strollers; Child craft, Simmons, and Bellini cribs; and Fisher Price, Little Tykes, and Playskool toys are accepted. Plan ahead as clothing is accepted roughly four to six months in advance of the season.

Don't forget tax write-offs. Explore neighborhood thrift shops, churches, temples, and the Salvation Army (call 757-2311 for a pickup appointment).

CHAPTER 3

Oopsy Daisy

CHILD SAFETY

When it comes to your child's safety, "when you least expect it, expect it" is the basic tenet of parenthood.

As a parent of a New York City tot, being overprepared is critical. It's knowing everything about everything: how to find a latch for a toilet that's older than your great grandmother, how to find the right CPR class, where to get infant Tylenol at 2:00 A.M. and how to get in touch with a poison control center without thinking twice.

Babyproofing

Every parent eagerly awaits the turning points when their child first crawls, pulls up, and walks. In New York, each of these milestones brings new hazards for children and new fears for parents. In the average New York City apartment, absolutely nothing is off limits to the average one-year-old. From the refrigerator to the toilet to the oven to the elevator, one small step for baby creates one giant fear for parentkind. Most of the big paraphernalia stores such as Albee's, Baby Palace, and Schneider's carry a broad range of safety equipment for do-it-yourselfers. However, there are also some great companies to help you to accomplish the seemingly difficult task of creating a safe environment for your child.

A good house is a safe house with the following:

➡ **Bumper pad for tables**

➡ **Cabinet locks**

➡ **Toilet latches**

➡ **Plug covers**

➡ **VCR insert**

➡ **Stove guards**

➡ **Tiny tot mace** (just joking)

➡ **Window guards**

➡ **Tub spout safety cover/mats**

➡ **Door/terrace lock guards**

➡ **Door gates**

➡ **Syrup of ipecac**

Perfectly Safe Catalogue
800-837-KIDS

This catalogue provides the opportunity to make your home
perfectly safe without ever leaving it. It offers a multitude
of safety items for infant to preschool needs. The items
range from infant wedges (that keep babies on their side
while sleeping) to outlet covers.

Child Proofers Inc.
366-5132

If you have a hard time envisioning yourself crawling on all
fours to spot potential hazards from a baby's eye view, call
in the experts. Child Proofers will make a house call free
of charge. They will evaluate your apartment, going room
to room, leaving no stone unturned, and finding every safety

hazard imaginable. Who knew how unsafe your grandmother's grandfather clock could be? They provide and install all the safety goods within a few days. The average cost is about $250, which is a lot cheaper than a trip to the emergency room.

SafetyNest Childproofing, Inc.
800-318-0030
703-379-7030

Donna Kurzbard Blair owns this comprehensive agency, which offers three distinct services. For the truly safety-conscious, spend $50 and she'll do a private home visit to give it a complete overhaul. She covers all safety issues including planning a fire escape route, identifying potential poisons, and evaluating each room (which may rock your decorating boat). For those do-it-yourselfers, a mere $15 will buy you a safety kit that lists general home hazards and how to remedy them. And, for those who find safety in numbers, gather up four of your friends and have a group workshop (more valuable than a Tupperware party).

CPR Instruction

No matter how well prepared you are, bad things can and sometimes do happen (please knock on wood). Among its many attributes, however, New York City boasts numerous quality healthcare professionals that can help you turn potentially hazardous situations into amusing cocktail party conversations.

In addition to the private instructors below, several area hospitals and program centers offer classes. Your pediatrician is a great reference for finding a program close to you.

Fern Drillings/Private CPR Instructor
744-6649

Fern will give group CPR instruction at neighborhood pediatricians' offices. The three-hour quickie class offers the basics for $50/session. Call her for available sessions in your area.

Save A Tot
Pediatric Associates
317 East 34th Street
725-7477

Though the name sounds silly, the services offered are not. For anyone who is going to spend time with your child, the $60 class is worthwhile. They teach infant and toddler CPR and what to do in the event of poisoning, drowning, or choking. The class is taught monthly; call for a complete schedule.

All-Night Pharmacies

It's cold. It's rainy. It's inevitable. The only thing in your apartment that's radiating heat is your child's forehead. And you're out of infant Tylenol. Oopsy daisy. Don't worry—like you and your child, the city doesn't sleep.

Duane Reade Drugs can be a bright spot even in your darkest hours. However, they don't deliver after hours, so put on your robe and go. They are located as follows:

➡ 224 West 57th Street at Broadway (541-9708)

➡ 1279 Third Avenue at 74th Street (744-2668)

➡ 2465 Broadway between 91st and 92nd Street (799-3172)

➡ 485 Lexington Avenue at 47th Street (682-5338)

➡ 378 Sixth Avenue at Waverly Place (674-5357)

Nobody likes to discuss . . . shhh . . . diarrhea. But more often than not it rears its ugly head at 4 A.M.! The night—what's left of it, anyway—will be more tolerable if you've stocked up on the requisite fluid replacement products. Make sure you know well in advance where to get the easier-to-administer Pedialyte pops. When this was written, the only place we could find them was at Thriftway on 23rd Street between First and Second Avenues.

Staying in Touch

If your child is taking advantage of all that New York City has to offer, more time is being spent outside than in. Therefore, to keep your child safe, it is not enough to have all key and emergency phone numbers and information taped to your refrigerator door. It is just as likely that an accident will happen in a crowded park as it will in the privacy of your kitchen. The following are tips to help ensure that staying in touch is as easy as AT&T says it should be:

➡ Have a list of emergency numbers taped to the back of your stroller or in the diaper bag—include the pediatrician, poison control, your office, and a back-up adult.

➡ The number for poison control is POISONS (764-7667).

➡ Make certain you and any caregiver knows which emergency room you are supposed to go to. Map out the quickest route.

➡ Always leave emergency cab fare for any caregiver.

➡ Consider getting a beeper so you are never out of touch with your child's caregiver.

➡ Teach your child (and caregiver) your phone number, street address, and 911.

➡ Hair barrettes (and any other accessory) with your child's name on them are really cute but . . . a bad idea. Most children will respond to someone who calls them by name.

➡ Snap your fingers. That's just about how long it takes for your child to wander off. It sounds obvious, but never lose sight.

CHAPTER 4

Mostly Moms

SUPPORT FOR NEW PARENTS

If you're like the rest of us, you rarely come across something just for you—sans child. This chapter is stuffed with information that addresses a variety of issues you may face. Whether you're looking to vent frustrations, share experiences, eat a meal, discuss your psyche, or simply make friends, there's a place for you. A few organized moms' groups provide advice, support, a good lunch, and most important, stimulating adult conversation—caviar for new moms.

Some are just for moms; others are BYOB (bring your own baby). Some take place at trendy restaurants, others at group members' apartments, and still others meet on sacred soil—at your pediatrician's office. We've also included some places that run forums for information-starved parents.

Just Moms

F.E.M.A.L.E (Formerly Employed Mothers
At the Leading Edge)
688-3750
Sara Schiff

F.E.M.A.L.E. is a national nonprofit group for women who have climbed off of the corporate ladder to raise children.

The East and West Side chapters meet bimonthly in one another's apartments (no kids or husbands) to discuss relevant issues. Depending on the topic, there may be a guest speaker. Past speakers have included an organization expert (who couldn't use that?), someone from the Parenting Center at the Y, and a chiropractor to help with postpartum aches.

TriBeCa Working Mothers Network
526-2258

A new group started in November 1996 by Felicity Fridman. She got the idea from a friend who told her about a New Jersey group for working mothers. The group's purpose is to provide an opportunity for working mothers to get together to discuss shared experiences and issues about juggling work and family responsibilities. You can also find them on the Web at www.tribecaworkingmothers.com.

Meet, Greet, and Eat (BYOB)

New Mothers Luncheons
HI LIFE RESTAURANT
1340 First Avenue at 72nd Street
744-3194

These weekly gatherings are run by a vivacious woman named Ronni Soled and take place in a private room in the back of the restaurant (use the side entrance on First Avenue—it's stroller-friendly). You can count on circle games and fun for baby (newborn to one-year-old) and a guest speaker and lunch for mom. The speakers cover issues that are relevant and topical for new mothers. Subjects range from going back to work to child psychology. No reservation is required—just show up at 11:30 A.M. on Tuesdays and have fun.

New Mommies' Network
Upper West Side
769-3846

What started out as new mommies who lunch has turned into one-stop shopping for families. Lori Robinson hosts a dinner series for expectant moms on the Upper West side, too. New mommies luncheons (infants to one-year-olds), new mommy graduates class, and play center tours (ten months to twenty months old) are held at various restaurants, program centers, and play centers around the city. Between twenty to thirty-five new moms and their babies attend each event (dads are always invited). Get ready for boisterous affairs. There is usually a guest speaker discussing relevant topics.

Dr., Dr., Give Me the News

Parent Learning
West 11th Street Pediatrics
46 West 11th Street
353-1759

These informative group sessions are run by Joy Greenberg, a clinical social worker, and are open to anyone who is interested. Each group is comprised of approximately six new moms and their tots (birth to twelve months). The sessions run for six weeks. Joy facilitates discussions on topics of interest to new moms and supplements the sessions with articles and handouts.

Parenting Your Toddler
TriBeCa
966-3483

Vivian Farmery, a social worker, leads this group. She specializes in treating families and children. She runs groups for moms with newborns, moms with toddlers, and moms with older children. The toddler group covers topic areas such as "handling tantrums and the no stage," "setting limits," "separations," and "toilet-training strategies." Child-care is provided. Call for session dates, times, and location.

Dr. Barry Stein
1125 Park Avenue at 90th Street
289-1400

One of the many perks of signing your child on with Dr. Stein and his associates is a new mother's group he runs from his office. New moms begin their first group (usually consisting of six to eight moms) when their little one is five weeks old and continue as long as the group is interested. Topics discussed change as your child matures, but include things like eating, sleeping, wishing you were sleeping, and what to expect next.

Note: Check with your own pediatrician to see if he or she runs a new mothers' group. If not, encourage him or her to do so.

On the Way to the Forum

92nd Street Y
1395 Lexington Avenue between 91st and
92nd Streets
415-5611

The 92nd Street Y runs informational forums for parents. One of the best known is about preparing to enter the pre-school fray. These forums are held annually in the fall at the Y. Some say they provide the most objective information anywhere in New York on the preschool application and interviewing process. Most important, they give you advice on what preschool directors expect from parents. The Y's Parenting Center also holds many other forums on a variety of child-centered and new-parent topics. You can find out when the Y is running their next forum by calling them or watching for their notices in *New York Family* or *Big Apple Parents* magazines.

The Parents League of New York
115 East 82nd Street between Lexington and Park Avenues
737-7385

The Parents League offers a forum in the spring for parents interested in preschools and one in the fall for ongoing schools. Here, you can listen to those in the know, the nursery school directors, and hear their perspective on the admissions process. The Parents League also sponsors other forums for parents, which run the gamut of issues. You are welcome to attend these forums if you are a member of the Parents League. To join, just call them or visit their office Monday through Thursday between the hours of 9 A.M. and 4 P.M. or Fridays until noon.

The Rhinelander Children Center
350 East 88th Street between First and Second Avenues
423-0532

The Rhinelander holds informational sessions for parents. Engaging and intimate, these sessions give parents information on such things as building your child's self-esteem, how to teach your child right from wrong, and tips on managing more than one child. Parenting classes are held at their facility. Call for more information.

SoHo Parenting Center
568 Broadway, Suite 205
334-3744

This center offers workshops on, among other things, one of the most important issues we face—sleepless nights. It helps parents discover strategies for getting their babies to sleep through the night. Sign us up. Also, they offer counseling and mothers groups.

Central Park Playground Partners
315-0385
Contact: Lexi Peyer at extension 24

A program of the Women's Committee of the Central Park Conservancy, this group raises money to equip a crew and vehicle to make routine and special repairs to all playgrounds. The crew repairs all play equipment and works to rid the playgrounds of rodents. Playground Partners enlists help from the community in the form of playground captains who, along with the crew, coordinate community clean-ups. They also equip each playground with a bulletin board of up-to-date helpful information.

Just Say Cheese

Andrea Wolff Photography
Hand-tinted portraits
979-7199

Literally hundreds of children's photographers are scattered in the city, but Andrea's work is remarkable. She combines a craftsman's skill with an artist's inspiration to create one-of-a-kind timeless portraits of your children. She shoots beautiful black-and-white photography and then hand-paints the images. With Andrea, you are bound to have portraits that will be aesthetically pleasing to more than just you and your mother-in-law.

A Hairy Situation

Berenice Electrolysis & Beauty Center
29 East 61st Street between Madison and
Park Avenues
355-7055

We won't fess up as to which one of us grew the postpartum mustache. However, we do know she is not alone. Berenice's is the best place to conduct the clandestine removal of unwanted, unsightly, I-can't-believe-this-happened-to-*me* hair. She loves it if you bring your kids along (pack some toys or coloring books) while you get some relatively pain-free expert electrolysis. Berenice is the hair removal guru to the mustached (sometimes bearded) Manhattan moms. She even keeps a photo album of all the tots who are in part responsible for this unwanted phenomenon.

CHAPTER 5

What a Classy Town

PROGRAMS

By the time your child is nine months, you won't be able to escape the park bench chatter about children's programs. It goes something like this, "So . . . where are you taking her?" "How did *you* get in *there*?" and "Oh . . . you're not doing *anything*? That's interesting."

Whether you want your child booked every day or just once a week, there's a program out there to nurture your child's creative genius and to fit your scheduling needs. The city is plastered with them—they're jammed into every nook and cranny. The class offerings run the gamut from art appreciation to Olympic gymnastics.

The programs listed in this chapter are among the best we've tried ourselves or heard about from others. Regardless of which programs you choose, consider the following:

➡ **Parent/child or caregiver/child classes.** Several centers make this designation.

➡ **Application deadline.** Believe it or not, a nine-month-old can get shut out of Tumbling 101.

➡ **Length of class.** Most of the under-twos can handle no more than one hour.

➡ **Number of children per class.** Remember to double the

number to include the adults (boy, it can get a little too cozy in some places).

➡ **Your child's nap schedule.** While you may have snoozed through Psych 101, it's not a good idea here.

➡ **Location.** It often makes more sense to stay close to home.

➡ **Prices.** You can end up spending $400 per session (usually about seventeen weeks) for a forty-five minute class that meets once a week.

One-Stop Playing

No need to hop on the bus at 9 A.M. on Monday, take the E train Wednesdays at noon, or walk twenty-five blocks each Friday to take your child to a variety of fun classes; in most neighborhoods you can have it all in one place. Throughout the city well-rounded program centers offer an array of classes including music, movement, arts & crafts, swimming, cooking, dance, story time, and combination classes for older tots. While these centers offer many things to do, we're featuring some highlights. Call these centers for information on session dates, fees, and class offerings.

Asphalt Green
555 East 90th Street at York Avenue
369-8890

Come here if you're looking for small, mixed age group classes. There is plenty to do here with buildings and playing fields set on over five acres—rare in Manhattan. Classes run the gamut from art to gymnastics to pre-ballet to weekend pee-wee soccer.

The Chelsea Piers Sports and Entertainment Complex
23rd Street and 12th Avenue
336-6200, 6500

What a workout! This mega complex offers a variety of toddler programs. With options such as preschool gymnastics, Pier Play, ballet, soccer, and rock climbing, one may consider docking a houseboat and never leaving the pier.

92nd Street Y
1395 Lexington Avenue between 91st and
92nd Streets
415-5611

Join their Parenting Center for discounted pricing and priority registration. Among other excellent classes, the world famous Parkbench program is an excellent introduction to a classroom setting. Also, try their Kids in the Kitchen if you need another chef in the apartment.

Rhinelander Children's Center
350 East 88th Street between First and
Second Avenues
876-0500

In the prettiest brownstone on the block, they offer a pre-school alternative program starting at two years eight months and computer classes for three-year-olds. And remember art is the ticket here but classes fill up quickly, so be sure to inquire early.

74th Street Magic
510 East 74th Street between York Avenue
and the River
737-3070

Big, bright, and airy, this space has every piece of gym equipment imaginable. Don't be fooled by the big gym, however; they offer lots of other activities running the gamut from cooking to arts & crafts.

Rhythm & Glues
1520 York Avenue at 80th Street
734-0922

This bright, cheery atmosphere offers programs starting at six months. As its name implies, your child can dance and sing and then paint and glue in rapid succession. It doesn't get much better than that. They also offer classes that are designated for parents or caregivers.

Elliott's Gym
65 West 70th Street between Central Park West and Columbus Avenue
595-0260

More than its name implies, Elliott's Gym is an excellent all-around program. While grown-ups may feel like they're in a doll house, your child will feel right at home with everything to scale—small scale that is. Even the student/teacher ratio is small at five to one.

Sol Goldman YM-YWHA of the Educational Alliance
344 East 14th Street between First and Second Avenues
780-0800

The Parenting and Family Center here offers a nice array of unique and targeted programs to meet the needs of the entire family. With such offerings as Mellow Monday for three years old and under, New Parent Stroll-in, Me and My Dad, and Employed Mothers Group, it definitely won't feel like the same old thing at this newly refurbished building.

Discovery Programs
251 West 100th Street at West End Avenue
749-8717

The granola approach to your child's first program—relaxed, friendly, and child-focused. You might be lynched if you don your Gucci loafers here. A sampling of classes include everything from forty-five–minute music, art, and ballet (parent or caregiver must attend) to a two-hour separation program.

Hop, Skip, and a Jump

This is about all it takes to get from one end of your apartment to the other. Children need a safe and roomy place to flex their gross motor muscles. Most of these classes offer your child a colorful padded environment, lots of age-appropriate gym equipment, and a spunky instructor to motivate and inspire them through it all.

Gymboree
5 locations throughout Manhattan
308-6353 (main office)

Gymboree offers several fun programs for children between three months and three years. Each forty-five–minute class involves both structured and unstructured activities, including music and gym. The environment is very bright, clean, and cheerful. Longer, more diversified classes are offered for children eighteen months and older.

Jodie's Gym
244 East 84th Street between Second and Third Avenues
772-7633

Your child will enjoy tumbling in this brightly colored and spacious gym; you, however, may be put off by the four-story trip in the freight elevators with lots of women checking one another out. Your child gets to maneuver through various gymnastic stations so she can decide early which piece of equipment she prefers for Olympic competition.

Gymtime Gymnastics Center
1520 York Avenue at 80th Street
861-7732

Perfect tiny replicas of adult gymnastic equipment, this spacious gym is glass enclosed so your in-laws can peek in at your little Mary Lou Retton. York Avenue Preschool's classrooms wrap around the gym, so those students, too, can peek in if their ABCs get a little boring.

Columbus Gym
606 Columbus Avenue between 89th and 90th Streets
721-0090

For those with real athletic prowess, Columbus Gym offers big kid gym classes for little tots. Children can improve their coordination through the obstacle courses, rings, and hoola hoops. The massive trampoline, which the whole class uses at the same time, offers a fantastic lesson in group dynamics. Your child is bound to be both at the bottom and top of the pack in a single bounce. They also have a nice preschool alternative program.

Sutton Gymnastics
20 Cooper Square, Third Avenue at Fifth Street
533-9390

Your eighteen-month-old can start honing her gross motor skills in this beautiful, bright loft. If she gets hooked on this gymnastics program with its excellent instructor and new equipment, she can stay on here practically forever, learning new skills and keeping her eye on the Olympics.

Sokol Gymnastics
420 East 71st Street between York and First
Avenues
861-8206

Sokol New York was founded in 1867. The Czechoslovakian immigrants brought this movement with them to the U.S. and continue to uphold the motto "A Sound Mind in a Healthy Body." They offer pre-tot gymnastics for ten-month-olds. We guess they mean infant gymnastics.

Circus Gym
2121 Broadway at 74th Street
799-3755

A really, really *happy* place where you can spend forty minutes with your six-month-old singing, moving, and grooving. The staff is well qualified to teach gymnastics. The space is sun-flooded and huge. Junior gymnastics begins at age three.

Children's Tumbling
9-15 Murray Street near City Hall
233-3418

Your child's athletic training can begin at the entrance as he pushes the large swinging doors of the freight elevator. Once upstairs, however, the focus is on developing basic movement and gymnastic skills for the two-and-up crowd.

Children's Athletic Training School
593 Park at 64th Street
751-4876
236 West 73rd Street between Broadway and
Amsterdam
877-3154

A real athletic program for children, the early focus here is on developing gross motor skills while enjoying a group activity. The little ones get to do things like hit koosh balls with hockey sticks and run from one end of the gym to the other to find objects hidden under regulation game cones. A great place to familiarize your child with the smell, feel, and taste of playing sports. Sign up early here!

Tippy Toes

You'll be hooked the first day you watch a Ballet for Two's class. After all, who could possibly resist the sight of pink leotard and tights straining to cover that puffy diapered tush? You may, however, find it easy to resist the sound of tiny tap shoes scratching your hardwood floors.

Manhattan Ballet School Inc.
149 East 72nd Street between Third and
Lexington Avenues
535-6556

The school's director, Elfriede Merman (née von Busse Grapputo) trained in Germany and has danced all over the world. She has taught ballet for over twenty years. This school is for girls beginning at age two-and-a-half years, so long as your little sophisticate is toilet trained and able to separate.

Ballet Academy East
1651 Third Avenue between 92nd and 93rd Streets
410-9140

This versatile school offers mother/child movement class for two-year-olds who are dressed for *Swan Lake*—full "pinks" are required. Although it's called "movement," they do learn some real stuff—passé, relevé, and the unique ballerina curtsy. Pre-ballet, tap, and Isadora Duncan Dance technique begin at age three.

Kids Co-Motion
579 Broadway between Prince and Houston Streets
65 West 86th Street and Amsterdam Avenue
431-8489

You both can learn a twirl or two here. The downtown class, housed in a professional dance studio, has an inspiring air of authenticity. But, sorry, when he is three-and-a-half, you don't get to go with him anymore.

Alvin Ailey American Dance Center
211 West 61st Street Third Floor between
Amsterdam and West End Avenue
767-0940

Alvin Ailey's First Steps Program may well be your child's first step towards a professional dance career. The focus here isn't on fluff and tutus but rather on achieving attainable and purposeful goals. While the curriculum is serious, the attitude is fun and inspiring—who knew that jumping like a frog at three could some day lead to leaping across the stage at Lincoln Center?

Steps on Broadway
2121 Broadway at 74th Street
874-2410

No diaper-stuffed leotards here. The pre-dance program begins at age four. And good things come to those who wait: ballet and tap classes aren't offered until first grade. The environment is truly inspiring with its big airy studios and grown-up ballerinas to ogle.

Perichild Program
132 Fourth Avenue at 13th Street, 2nd Floor
505-0886

Perichild offers classes ranging from creative ballet to tae kwon do. And the nice thing is that your child can watch professional dance troupes who practice here and participate in a real performance of their own.

Splish Splash
Only so much fun can be had in the bath. Then, its time to move on to bigger and better splashes. There are several well-maintained and cheerful pools around the city that offer adult/child classes. Many of these aquatic classes are innovative and fun.

Asphalt Green
555 East 90th Street at York Avenue
369-8890

One of the newest, splashiest, coolest pools in the city. At times, it can be overwhelming when four different school swim teams are practicing in the big pool. Fortunately, they have a separate little pool for your little swimming tot. They also offer swim classes for children with special needs.

West Side YMCA
5 West 63rd Street between Central Park West
and Broadway
787-4400

While they offer exercise and art classes here, the swimming program stands out. Gorgeous, deep sea-blue Spanish tiling lines the walls of this pool. The instructors are warm and friendly and are able to coax just about any reluctant tot (or parent) into scooping and kicking up a storm. Feel free to say no to any of their suggestions like "how about your little guppy going under water?" They won't be offended.

92nd Street Y
1395 Lexington Avenue between 91st and
92nd Streets
415-5611

They offer private, semiprivate, and group lessons for tots. At age three, your child can start in the Learn to Swim program. You may remember your own early swim years as your child receives Red Cross certification as she completes each level.

Swim Tots
131 West 86th Street between Columbus and
Amsterdam Avenues
787-3356

What a surprise to find a pool in this building. Classes start at six months and by the time the tots are two, they'll be as proficient as little ducks.

Vanderbilt YMCA
224 East 47th Street between Second and
Third Avenues
756-9600

The chance of your child's getting hit by a butterflyer here
is nil; the west pool is for kid classes only. Classes start at
six months, but from three years on up, children learn real
swimming skills. No need to worry about goose bumps
here, the pool for first timers is nice and warm.

53rd Street YWCA
610 Lexington Avenue at 53rd Street
735-9702

A handy location if you want to meet your tot for a swim
on your lunch hour, this Y boasts a great pool for new pad-
dlers.

They're Playing Our Song

Most expectant parents dream of singing songs with their
adoring child. Then reality sets in. After you realize that your
repertoire of songs at best includes three, you'll need to look
elsewhere for inspiration. If you fall into this category, don't fret.
There are many wonderful classes in which you can share the
magic of music with your child. Some program centers offer in-
strumental lessons, which can provide some accompaniment to
your living room concerts.

Lucy Moses School for Music and Dance
129 West 67th Street between Broadway and
Amsterdam Avenues
501-3360

Within steps of Lincoln Center, this place is sure to inspire
the young artist in your child. This school is very well run
and a fun place to learn to love the arts. Classes, starting

as early as eighteen months, include keyboard together, sing together, and art together. All together now!

The Early Ear
48 West 68th Street between Central Park West and Broadway
877-7125

There's nothing like the real thing. In this unique set-up your child can touch and try real instruments. Children can enjoy the accompaniment of a pianist and violinist in the class while playing along on their own scaled down versions of the instruments. The little violins are so cute. The environment is intimate and comfortable (complete with a big sofa to lounge on, but no napping please).

Kindermusic
339 East 84th Street
120 West 76th Street
864-2476

For Gymboree graduates, this is a fun-filled music program for children starting at eighteen months. An instructor leads the children through a very structured, musical class where they will bang on instruments and sing-along. And the staff won't skip a beat if your unstructured little one wanders out of the circle.

Music Together
Upper East Side: 244-3046
West Side: 473-9594
Village: 366-1612
Battery Park City: 255-9227

This high quality program actually offers young ones the opportunity to use rhythm (never mind if the method didn't work for you). Don't despair if she is singing "Twinkle, Twinkle" before she says "Ma, Ma." In addition to music in the class, they give you tapes and songbooks to play and sing along with at home.

The Diller-Quaile School of Music
24 East 95th Street between Madison and Fifth
Avenues
369-1484

This quintessential music school features music and art, music and movement, or just plain music. They offer separation classes, which are the equivalent of a preschool alternative program (a perfect transition for pre-preschoolers). The staff is incredibly well qualified in music, art, and child development. Your young one can start Suzuki lessons as early as age three. Classes are a full year and you must apply about nine months in advance.

MaryAnn Hall's Music for Children
2 East 90th Street between Madison and
Fifth Avenues
800-633-0078

Connecticut based Maryann is the news here. With over twenty-four years worth of experience and quite a resume to boot, she writes all the music and material used in the classes. No chance of hearing old camp songs here. In this year-long program, classes start when your child is ten months, and each year is designed to build upon the previous one.

Turtle Bay Music School
244 East 52nd Street between Second and
Third Avenues
753-8811

And you taught your child that "Orff" was what the dog said. Well, after your eighteen-month-old finishes one Tuneful Tots class he'll know that it's really a fun method of learning about music. With an emphasis on learning music through movement and the use of really cool instruments, your child will become familiar with the fundamentals of rhythm, scales, and harmony.

School for Strings
419 West 54th Street between Ninth and
Tenth Avenues
315-0915

If your budding Beethoven is itching to play at three, this is one of the few places that will start him on the piano this young. This is a serious music program for both you and your child. Your child is expected to attend one private and two group classes per week. Be prepared. Your attendance is expected at a separate class where you learn to understand your little Beethoven's joys and frustrations. Violin and cello are also taught.

Greenwich House Music School
46 Barrow Street
242-4770

Located in a beautiful brownstone, Greenwich House offers visual and performing arts for children. Medley of the Arts for two-year-olds combines music and art for children and their parents/caregivers. By age three, your child is learning solfege (scales) and music theory through music, games, movement, and dance.

Third Street Music Settlement
235 East 11th Street between Second and
Third Avenues
777-3240

More than a century old and no longer on Third Street, this center provides an excellent variety of classes in the arts including music, dance, and painting. They really listen to parents here as the program has evolved based on the needs of the community. Their program includes parent/child classes for the nearly twos, separation classes for two-and-a-half-year-olds as well as a morning preschool.

Church Street School for Music and Arts
74 Warren Street between West Broad and
Greenwich Streets
571-7290

It's all in the process here. Imaginative props such as parachutes, scarves, and hoops are used as aids in teaching scales and other music theory concepts. Using clay, paint, collage, and her fingers, your little one is sure to create art projects that will be proudly displayed on your refrigerator.

Drop on By
OK, so you don't have to sign up for everything. There are places that offer great drop-in classes. Here, with little or no notice you can drop in to paint, play, or meet your friends.

The Chelsea Piers Sports and
Entertainment Complex
23rd Street and Hudson River
336-6200, 6500

What better to do on a Friday night or Sunday morning than attend an Open Gym/Rock session? A little pricey, but then again so is a trip to Montana.

Children's Museum of the Arts
72 Spring Street between Broadway and Lafayette
941-9198

A fun and funky space, your little one can drop in (with you, of course) and paint up a storm with tons of materials on hand and plenty of atmosphere to inspire.

Guggenheim SoHo
575 Broadway at Prince Street
423-3587

Once a month, you and your child can learn about art just for art's sake. At the SoHo Tots program, a nice peruse around the museum is followed up with a fun project including art and storytelling. Call ahead to sign up for each class.

Nelson A. Rockefeller Park
Battery Park City
267-9700

May through October is free drop-in time here. Stop in for preschool art projects and a view to boot. The classes usually take place in the pavillion. If you don't see them at first, ask around. Someone is *bound* to have noticed a large group of organized two-year-olds.

Rain or Shine
115 East 29th Street between Park and
Lexington Avenues
532-4420

A tropical forest replete with elephants and giraffes and birds—OK, so they're all part of the murals on the walls. No matter. Your tot can make use of Rain or Shine's spa-

cious art room to create a painting, hear some stories or
sing-a-long, take a romp 'n roll class, and then pop out to
the sandbox to blow off some steam.

My Favorite Place
265 West 87th Street between Broadway and
West End Avenues
362-5320

The upstairs arts & crafts room is the place to be when class
is in session. Your child will feel this is his favorite place
after he uses all of their creative and imaginative art supplies (and after he ropes you into buying him something on
the way out). Beware of the store you must pass through
before you can enjoy this place.

Playspace
2473 Broadway at 92nd Street
769-2300

Although a little pricey, if you wrap "free" play around these
classes, your budding thespian can act up in the Olympic-
sized sandbox after drama class.

CHAPTER 6

Stop Humming the Crimson Fight Song, She's Only Two

PRESCHOOL PREP

Contrary to popular belief, preschool acceptance is not the defining moment in your child's education. However, it may very well be the defining moment for your mental and physical well being for the next few months.

In an effort to preempt headaches and ulcers, on the morning you decide to tackle the preschool *issue*, do look at yourself straight on in the mirror and recite the following:

➡ I will not call my spouse and rant and rave about his/her defective family tree.

➡ I will not berate myself for not pursuing a career as chairman of the New York Stock Exchange.

➡ I will resist the urge to call my ex-roommate, whom I hated, to write a recommendation for my child at her child's school.

➡ I will not let this process swing my moods.

➡ I will not throw in the towel and move to Connecticut.

All set? OK. Here it is. We've divided this up in two parts. The first describes your child's schooling options. The second lays out the process, step by step.

Schooling Options

Two things to consider are 1) what is your child's age on the first of September, and 2) whether or not you want a nursery, ongoing school, or preschool alternative program.

YOUR CHILD'S AGE

Discussing your child's age as of September 1 with admissions directors will leave you befuddled unless you understand their lingo: "2.4" as of September 1 means your child is two years and four months old. It's important that you check with each preschool as to their cutoff date. But don't worry if you forget. When you call for an application, it's one the first things they'll ask you.

SCHOOL TYPE

Broadly speaking, there are three types of preschool situations:

➡ **Nursery or preschool.** Starts at about age two-and-a-half and continues through pre-K.

➡ **Ongoing schools.** Some start at age three or four and continue through elementary school (or beyond).

➡ **Preschool alternative programs.** Usually held at program centers (e.g., Diller-Quaille and Rhinelander), preschool alternative classes have a separation component and are usually longer (one-and-a-half hours) than toddler classes. Many parents, who do not want to send their child to preschool until age three or have missed the age cutoff, choose this route for their two-year-olds or young threes.

The Process
(To get in the mood, think Vivaldi's "Four Seasons.")

SPRING

1. The first step is to determine which schools you are going to call in September. Start looking in your neighborhood, as convenience is one of the most important factors to consider. Ask neighbors with older kids for their advice. At this stage, cast a wide net—consider lots of schools and be open-minded. Two great sources are the *Manhattan Directory of Private Nursery Schools* by Linda Faulhaber and The Parents League of New York.

SUMMER

2. Try to forget about the whole preschool thing for two months. Enjoy the sun. Splash around. Don't forget the sunblock. Reality check should occur around mid-August. Hey, the summer's almost over anyway. If you picked the schools you're interested in at step one, skip to step three. If not, pick them now.

FALL

3. Most schools take phone requests for applications the day after Labor Day for admission the following September. Make sure you can hit redial, as busy signals are not uncommon. But, if you don't get through, don't fret, there is always the day after.

4. As a rule of thumb, most applications are due in December or January. Be organized. Make a chart. Since deadlines vary by school, pay attention. No excuses accepted here!

5. Apply to at least three to five schools, keeping in mind the application fees and the number of interviews you want you and/or your child to participate in. Even though you know any school would be lucky to have your child, admissions

result from a somewhat random process. Increase your chances of admission and give yourself a few options.

6. Tour scheduling also varies by school. Many schools require that you apply before you take the tour. Nevertheless, take the tours seriously. First impressions (yours, not theirs) are often the most important. Try to ask good questions. But remember, there is a fine line between inquisitive and annoying. And don't forget, a picture speaks a thousand words; keep your eyes peeled for:

➡ **The walls.** Is it a colorful, stimulating environment?

➡ **The staff.** Are the teachers warm, nurturing, and interacting with the children?

➡ **Outdoor space.** Is there fun, outdoor equipment? Try to envision your child two years from now, and a lot bigger, playing in that space.

➡ **Indoor play.** Is there any? Remember, it does rain.

7. Be sure to send thank-you notes to each school's tour guide. Common courtesy can't hurt. Also, try to include some specifics in your note, preferably things you liked about the school.

WINTER

8. The interview process varies by school (e.g., group play, one-on-one, parental). Whatever you do, don't stress over your child's unpredictable behavior. It's not worth it.

9. Right before your interview is a good time for letters of recommendations to be sent. Only people who are affiliated with the school in some way (an alum or parent of current/ former student) and who know your child should write them. But be prepared to send your child if accepted. There's an unwritten code of ethics on this issue.

10. If you have a clear first choice, it behooves you to write a

note after your child's interview declaring your love and devotion to that particular school (genuine, of course).

11. Most schools will notify you by early March. Notification is not unlike your college experience. Thick envelope means you're in (your child, that is), thin means you've been rejected or wait-listed.

12. If you are wait-listed, don't despair. It helps to pursue your favorite school. Be warned, the admissions directors talk to one another, so only tell one school that it's your top choice (this goes for step ten, too). Believe it or not, all children seem to get in somewhere.

Pre-School Prep
CHECKLIST

NAME OF SCHOOL	DATE APPLICATION REQUESTED	DATE APPLICATION RECEIVED	HEAD OF SCHOOL/ ADMISSIONS	TOUR DATE	CHILD INTERVIEW	PARENT INTERVIEW	LETTER OF RECOMMENDATION	THANK YOU NOTE	NOTES/ THOUGHTS
1.									
2.									
3.									
4.									
5.									

It Was a Bash,
It Was a Monster Bash!

BIRTHDAY PARTIES

The days of "pin the tail on the donkey" are long gone. Believe it or not, planning a child's birthday party for eight can take on the complexity of planning a wedding for 250. However, with advanced planning, adequate space, and age-appropriate, good entertainment (by kiddy standards, not yours), a birthday party can be a piece of cake. A few things to consider when planning a party are:

➡ **Location.** At home or at a facility (which usually requires booking about one to two months in advance).

➡ **Duration.** An hour and a half should suffice.

➡ **Food.** Don't feel obliged to have the party during mealtime; cake and drinks are enough at this age.

➡ **Entertainment.** Will you hire someone (again, this means you'll have to book one to two months in advance), just let the kids play, or display your own hidden talents?

➡ **Favors.** Oh the pressure!

➡ **Guest list.** Keep it short for your own sake as well as your child's.

- ➡ **Invitations.** Should be sent out at least two weeks in advance.

- ➡ **Perspective.** Have it or get it; it's only a birthday party.

Clowning Around

All you need for a ninety-minute at-home bash is thirty minutes of fun entertainment. While it is not absolutely necessary and will run you at least $200, it does take the burden off of you. Just witness one parent's failed attempt at musical chairs and you'll be on the phone booking a clown for your tot's party. While there are literally hundreds available, here are some entertainers worth calling:

Silly Billy
David Friedman
645-1299

Best suited for the over three crew, Silly Billy is oh, so-o-o silly. His inventive children's theater is great for the outgoing future thespian party-goers. He involves the children in acting out favorites such as *The Three Little Pigs* and makes costumes for each participant out of balloons as the story progresses. His magic tricks are also fun and involve the children, too. His biting commentary and "over the three-year-old head" jokes are a little Don Rickels-esque, but sure to elicit silly sounds from the adults.

Starmite Puppeteers
Barry Keating
473-3409

It's hard to find a great entertainer for two-year-olds that won't scare at least half the tots. Barry, who worked with the Muppets, is both engaging and entertaining. He is warm, endearing, and adaptable—frequently reaching into his big puppet bag, filled with all of your child's favorites, to switch gears if the kids are getting bored or antsy. He will spend time with parents in advance to ensure that the show meets the needs of your child.

Company's Coming
Mary Ellen Hostak
260-3036

Whether you opt for the Tinker Bell, Polka Dot Kid, or Fairy Princess–clad Mary Ellen, you are guaranteed to have the kids mesmerized. Her repertoire for the three and under set includes songs, puppets, and movement. The puppet show (performed in the open) has lots of variety and is friendly and engaging. The songs and movements are those familiar to the children so they feel comfortable joining in the fun. You may feel compelled to join in for a round of the Hokey Pokey.

Professor J. P. Putter
Scientist-Inventor-Magician
595-7023

Not your average absentminded type, this professor appeals to kids of all ages. Dressed in a wacky suit with a bow tie and funny shoes, Professor Putter weaves his magic spell with daring demonstrations of letters that float in the air, gadgets that produce water out of thin air, and an unending stream of streamers, which he pulls out of his mouth. He grabs all of his props out of a large steamer trunk and works behind a masking tape line that children are not allowed to cross. Professor Putter keeps up a constant patter of conversation peppered with lots of questions for his audience, which encourages every child to participate.

Pinkies Party Palace
718-822-7462

A cross between Pippy Longstocking and Tracy Ullman, Pinkie is that rare find, a performer that you'll find as amusing as the three-year-olds do. From pulling a hamster from a sock to a rabbit from a hat, the magic is mesmerizing. Children feel very comfortable participating in the show and the birthday child truly enjoys center stage.

Other Party People

In addition to party entertainers, consider the instructors at your child's program center as they will often do birthday parties. A familiar face can be worth a lot more than a life-sized Barney!

Let 'Em Eat Cake

Let's be honest, this is the part all partygoers look forward to (particularly the adults). A great dessert can obliterate any precake party disasters one might have. Lots of places offer delicious treats throughout the city, but the following are worth seeking out:

CBK of New York Cookies
226 East 83rd Street between Second and
Third Avenues
794-3383
366 Amsterdam Avenue between 77th and
78th Streets
787-7702

Specializing in made-to-order cakes (order one month in advance), cookies, and cupcakes, CBK bakes delicious sweets for toddler birthday parties. Their colorful cupcakes are yummy and a good substitute for cakes, which can be hard to handle for little ones. Each tot can have his own cupcake and enjoy utensil-free dining without offending Emily Post. They will spell out H-A-P-P-Y B-I-R-T-H-D-A-Y and your child's name on the cupcakes for a fun-to-eat treat. Just make sure no one samples the H before the party.

Cupcake Café
522 Ninth Avenue at 39th Street
465-1530

This bakery lives up to its reputation for having the best cakes in town. The cakes are both fabulously creative and deliciously scrumptious. This is one of life's situations where you actually get what you wish for. If you request a cake that looks like Darth Vadar, be prepared for ominous. They do not deliver, but it is worth the trip.

Eileen's Cheesecakes
17 Cleveland Place across from the Spring Street
Train (6) Station
966-5585

For the more sophisticated palate, Eileen is reputed to have the best cheesecake and chocolate mousse cake in the city. With the requisite Disney character decorations on top, you won't feel like your child is missing out just because you are getting the ultimate taste sensation. Even more appetizing is delivery anywhere in the city for just $1.00.

Greenberg's
1100 Madison Avenue between 82nd and
83rd Streets
744-0304

Greenberg's, with five locations, has cakes that are delicious and dairy kosher. They offer made-to-order birthday cakes in the shape of your child's favorite character. Local delivery is available. They recommend ordering the cakes two weeks in advance.

Madison Avenue's Better Baker
1006 Madison Avenue between 77th and
78th Streets
396-0001

It's the icing on the cake. Fat-free on the outside, lowfat on the inside, these cakes will have parents asking for more. Children will never know the difference because the cakes look like the real McCoy decorated with their favorite characters. Just let them know what you want at least three days in advance.

Soutine
104 West 70th Street between Broadway and
Columbus Avenue
496-1450

Bring your favorite picture and don't worry about the impact on your wallet. Soutine will decorate junior's cake anyway he'd like it. Don't be put off by the French name; the prices are quite reasonable.

Do Me a Favor

If you are not up for making the little bags yourself, several stores will put together great favors (candy-free) with age-appropriate trinkets for the party guest. Surprisingly, these don't necessarily cost an arm and a leg. Examples include the following:

➡ **Cozy's Cuts for Kids.** 1125 Madison Avenue (744-1716)/ 448 Amsterdam Avenue (579-2600).

➡ **My Favorite Place.** 265 West 87th Street (362-5320).

➡ **Ben's for Kids.** 1380 Third Avenue (794-2330).

- **Kidding Around.** 60 West 15th Street (645-6337).
- **Fun by the Basket.** 1349 Lexington Avenue (289-5960).

Also keep in mind that you do not have to spend a bundle on favors (a well-hung sack can cost up to $10). Consider single items, which can be more useful and memorable such as:

- Little books
- Cute place mats
- Bouncy balls (obviously not bite-sized)
- Crayons and coloring books
- Mini playdough
- Stickers
- Mini puzzles
- Finger puppets

All Decked Out

No need to hyperventilate or to run to the D & D building. It's a children's party. But do pick a theme (jungle, Batman, ballet)—it makes your life easier—and don't overdo it.

E.A.T. Gifts
1062 Madison Avenue between 80th and
81st Streets
861-2544

If you didn't already splurge on other party paraphernalia, try this store for great favors, paper goods, decorations, and invitations. The store is such a feast for the eyes that a perusal of the cake decorations and baking accessories makes even the most ardent bake-a-phobic tempted to do it the old fashioned way—in your own kitchen with a Betty Crocker mix. Their cake toppers will make any cake (no matter how lopsided) look delicious.

Golden's
2512 Broadway between 93rd and 94th Streets
749-3100

Primarily an art and stationery store, Golden's has every imaginable variety of balloons and crêpe paper—the decorating essentials for a birthday party. Make sure you order the balloons three days in advance so you're not kept waiting.

The Paper House
678 Broadway between 3rd and Bond Streets
388-0082
1370 Third Avenue at 78th Street
879-2937
269 Amsterdam Avenue between 72nd and
73rd Streets
724-8085
180 East 86th Street between Third and
Lexington Avenues
410-7950
1020 Third Avenue between 60th and 61st Streets
223-3774

If you need balloons blown without advanced warning, this store can do it on the spot. In addition to balloons, they carry most party supplies including invitations and paper goods.

Penny Whistle Toys
448 Columbus Avenue between 81st and
82nd Streets
873-9090
1283 Madison Avenue between 91st and
92nd Streets
369-3868

This store, as we mention in the Toys chapter, has *lots* of bins filled with inexpensive fun gifts.

Party Places

"Clean up, clean up, everybody everywhere, clean up, clean up, not my place so I don't care." Not necessarily a philosophy you want to impart to your child, but a really good reason to have a party elsewhere. The out-of-home party can be a great option for the space and time impaired. Some places will take care of just about everything from invitations to parting favors. The following is a sampling of party places scattered throughout the city:

Madison Avenue's Better Baker
1006 Madison Avenue between 77th and
78th Streets
396-0001

For most New York City children, just spending time in a big commercial kitchen is novel enough. But throw in some kiddy chefs hats and aprons, mini cookie cutters, confetti, and balloons and you have the ingredients for a delicious birthday party. This all-inclusive baking party is well planned—no waiting for oven timers. Children decorate prebaked cookies while the cookies they've cut are baking. On top of it all, they get birthday cake and gift bags to take out. Yum, yum.

My Favorite Place
265 West 87th Street between West End Avenue and
Broadway
362-5320

Their basement-like room gives you that at-home party feel without the fuss. The Toddler Playroom is yours for two hours along with two helpers to "facilitate play." No big Barney or Clown are necessary as the playroom boasts all your child's favorite toys and will provide ample fun for the two and under set. You can bring your own cake and pizza or they will arrange it for a fee. For the two-and-up crowd, the upstairs arts & crafts room is available at the same cost.

Grove Street Theater
Miss Magesties Lolipop Playhouse
39 Grove Street
741-6436

Not at all your suburban birthday. In fact, your friends in
Scarsdale will make the trip for this one. Miss Magesties
provides an opportunity for your child to be center stage
for his birthday. At birthday parties here, children get to
watch the original shows (see Kiddy Kulture for more details) and then jump up to the stage for some cake and a
happy birthday tune from the cast. In spite of its being a
great New York find, it's reasonably priced.

Jeremy's Place
322 East 81st Street between First and
Second Avenues
628-1414

Don't worry if your video camera runs out after just ten
minutes—you can count on Jeremy to take care of just
about everything. He will host and house your party, provide party bags, pizza, and cake; connect you with one of
the best children's entertainers (he doesn't do the whole
gig); videotape the whole thing; and let the kids see themselves on TV.

New York City Fire Museum
278 Spring Street between Hudson and
Varick Streets
691-1303

"When I grow up I wanna be a fireman" is a statement made
by many four-year-olds. Well, there's no need to wait if you
opt for a party here. These parties, held in a beautiful spacious loft atop the museum, are billed as fun and educa-

tional. There's free play time in a cute and colorful matted area, a gathering where children read an age-appropriate story and learn about safety (all will leave remembering stop, drop, and roll), an art project where they paint and decorate their own fire truck to take home, a scavenger hunt and visit with a real fireman in gear, Simon Says with a firehouse theme, music, and a themed cake. Wow, what more could the little chief ask for? All leave with a favor bag filled with treats such as a fireman's hat, stickers, and a badge.

The Children's Museum of the Arts
274-0986

Most children love to glue, paint, cut, color, sketch, and make a mess. Just throw in a cake and you have the makings for a great birthday party. Children can enjoy free play in the wonderful interactive art and play areas and then settle down to an art project that they can take home. All this fun culminates in the brightly colored Wonder Theater where children sink their teeth into delicious cake. At the time of this writing, the museum was moving, so call ahead for the address.

The Carousel
Central Park
396-1010 ext.13

Pray for a sunny day and consider this unique-to-New York birthday party. The basic party package includes four rides per child, an hour-long picnic lunch, drinks, favors, balloons, and a host. Of course, there are add-ons to make it more like a carnival such as clowns, games, and face painting. You are also free to import your own entertainment. But you probably don't need the extras; the average three-year-old will think the ride and park surroundings are just fine and dandy. Rain dates are provided. Book about one month in advance.

Warner Brothers Studio Store
1 East 57th Street at Fifth Avenue
754-0305

Fly with Superman up to the party room, dine on pizza and birthday cake with Daffy, and pose with Sylvester. The environment is ripe for fantastical fun. Children can enjoy a photo session with their favorite character and don 3-D glasses for an interactive movie experience. You're guaranteed to hear lots of giggles of delight. Your child will have so much fun they won't need much more. In fact, you can probably leave the store without hearing, "Mommy, I want . . ." Th-th-th-that's all folks!

Other Party Places

Most indoor play areas and some gym class centers will also house a great party of carefree romping (see Programs and Indoor Playgrounds chapters for listings of these centers).

CHAPTER 8

New Threads for Your Little Emperor

CLOTHING/SHOE STORES

While there are at least two sides to the argument over rearing children in New York, there is one inarguable topic—New York is the best place to shop for kids!

There are literally hundreds of stores, so it's helpful to know where to shop for what. If you don't, you'll be so frustrated that you'll end up putting your child in something resembling the Emperor's new clothes.

Hip, Hipper, and Hippest

Sometimes having a baby is just like having a little doll to dress. That is, until your child starts to have fashion (forward or backward) frenzies of her own. Just remember, it doesn't have to be black to be hip. Head for these stores. They'll have what you're looking for.

Ibiza Kidz
42 University Place between 9th and 10th Streets
505-9907

"One for you, one for me" is a phrase you are sure to be uttering in this boutique, which houses both children's and women's clothing. The styles are very hip and fun and can

give a whole new meaning to mother/daughter dresses . . .
no gingham check or floral prints here.

Space Kiddets
46 East 21st Street between Park Avenue
and Broadway
420-9878

This store has a thrift shop feel, but don't be fooled. You'll
find a wonderful assortment of hip clothes, including racks
of great western wear—tiny cowboy boots, too! It's also
great for dress-up (baskets of glittery shoes). Brightly
painted furniture and toys tucked into nooks and crannies
round out the selection.

Barney's
660 Madison Avenue at 61st Street
826-8900

Everything at Barney's children's department is something
you'd like to own for your tot but not have to pay for. From
silver rattles to mom-like terry robes to birthday party
dresses to bathing suits, the merchandise is sophisticated,
hip, and fun. You'll almost wish it all came in adult sizes.
It's a great place for special gifts or occasions or to shop
with your mother. If your child is growing out of clothes
every other month, it's not the fiscally responsible place to
shop for everyday items. But . . . watch for their great end-
of-season sales! Check the co-op for shoes.

Peanut Butter and Jane
617 Hudson Street between Jane and
West 12th Streets
620-7952

The spilled jar (fake) of baby food on the counter says it
all. This shabby chic boutique is literally jammed (no pun

intended) with clothes, toys, stuff for dress-up, books, and coats. If you are a neat freak, don't come here. But if you love hunting for things, you'll love what you find.

Catimini
1284 Madison Avenue between 91st and
92nd Streets
987-0688

French designer clothes dotted with bears, bunnies, and mushrooms. Catimini color schemes are very sophisticated—cream and beige and gray and red. Beware: some of their designs are very puffy, so try them on your little one or you just might find that you have created the "Michelin Baby."

Greenstones
442 Columbus Avenue between 81st and
82nd Streets
580-4322

Greenstones, Too!
1184 Madison Avenue between 86th and
87th Streets
427-1665

The store on the West Side is bigger than its East Side sister, but they are happy to shuffle merchandise between them. Very hip, very French, and very fun-to-wear clothes can be found here. They have a great selection of snowsuits and unusual fall and spring jackets and capes. If you're in need of some quick fashion advice, they're more than happy to lend a hand.

Robin's Nest
1168 Lexington Avenue at 80th Street
737-2004

This tiny place is just about as big as a bird's nest. But their selection of stretchy pants and tops, bibs, receiving blankets, and handknit sweaters will leave you chirping. The gals who work here are incredibly nice and will help you pick out the perfect gift. Not for the short-of-time, their festive gift-wrapping is in a league all its own.

Julian & Sara
103 Mercer, corner of Spring Street
226-1989

It doesn't get much hipper than SoHo. Even though they carry many of the things you can get in uptown stores, it's much more fun to shop here. They stock Catimini and Deux par Deux, not to mention those really great Austrian boiled wool jackets.

ABC Carpet & Home
888 Broadway at 19th Street
473-3000

Located on the first floor (to your left as you walk into the store), ABC stocks a cache of hiphop clothes, toys, and baby furniture. They carry beautiful hand embroidered clothing by designers you may not have heard of. This is great for those who love to buy things that are not being worn by every Tom, Dick, or Harry. ABC's baby furniture has that wrought-iron, distressed wood sophistication that you only thought possible for adult furniture. A great gift buying stop, they specialize in toys that are antique or unusual (no Power Rangers).

Monkeys & Bears
506 Amsterdam Avenue between 84th and
85th Streets
873-2673

You won't need to weed through racks of stuff here. The carefully selected merchandise ranges from basic designers like Flapdoodle and City Lights to the more chic Marcel et Leon, Arthur Confiture, and Galipette. Their tasteful buyers can save *you* from having to be selective as it is all wonderful. Also wonderful is their jellyroll gift-wrapping. One caveat: the children's bookshelf is not necessarily for children. They don't take kindly to little hands pulling them all off the shelf.

Oilily
870 Madison Avenue between 70th and 71st Streets
628-0100

Put on your sunglasses and come on in. Wait a minute. This is New York and the clothes aren't black. Wait a minute. This is a children's store and there's no pale pink and blue. Welcome to Oilily. It's Dutch. It's funky. It's expensive.

Coco & Z
222 Columbus Avenue at 70th Street
721-0415

Named for its owners' children, Coco & Z definitely reflects the fact that its owned, managed, and operated by parents of young kids. The charming and unusual clothing is not only great looking and hip, but also practical and reasonably priced. And unlike those of many other specialty stores, their boys' selection is pretty strong.

The Classics

Think timeless smocking, fabulous stitching, and tailored lines. Although you usually pay more at these stores, there *really* is a chance your next one can wear it, too. And never forget there are half-price sales in January—plan ahead.

Au Chat Botte
1192 Madison Avenue between 87th & 88th Streets
722-6474

Walk in here and you will feel like you strolled off the Boulevard St. Germain. The staff all speak both French and English. Their designer clothes are French and Italian and gorgeous. Sumptuous smocking and beautiful, crisp colors. They also have everything for your layette needs.

Bonpoint
811 Madison Avenue at 68th Street
879-0900
1269 Madison Avenue at 91st Street
722-7720

The ultimate garments at the ultimate prices. While there is no denying Bonpoint's smocking is unparalleled, so too is what happens to your wallet when you leave here. Come here for very special party outfits or when your mother is treating.

Magic Windows
1186 Madison Avenue at 87th Street
289-0028

This store has an extensive selection of clothing and carries such designers as Florence Eisemann. They have the under-two apparel separated from the older kid's clothes for easier shopping. Lots of smocking (no surprise), but the prices are affordable (now, that *is* a surprise). Watch for their trunk shows.

Wicker Garden
1327 Madison Avenue between 93rd and
94th Streets
410-7001

Unlike any garden you've ever seen, this is a place you can browse to your heart's content. They have acres of clothes downstairs (including layette items) and furniture upstairs. Volumes of catalogues abound from which you can choose everything from cribs to armoires to nursery wallpaper. Not for the faint of wallet.

Spring Flowers
1050 Third Avenue at 62nd Street
758-2669
905 Madison Avenue between 72nd and
73rd Streets
717-8182

Even if you need to dress a little boy for a wedding, you are certain to find something precious and classic. They carry beautiful and expensive clothing and a wonderful selection of dress shoes (but no shoe salesmen). Your mother-in-law is sure to say "now . . . he looks so handsome."

What a Bargain

You don't come to these places for atmosphere. But the savings can be significant, and who doesn't love that? Be prepared to do some hunting and to come back some other time if they don't have what you came for. Also, these stores tend to be crowded or inconveniently located, so leave the kids at home or invite a friend to tag along. In general, the prices on all summer stuff get reduced in direct proportion to the Manhattan population. This summer sale rule applies to most stores in this chapter, not just to the bargains.

M. Kreinen Sales Corp.
301 Grand Street at Allen Street
925-0239

A Lower East Side institution and definitely not a store for browsing. But if you are on the prowl for pajamas and underwear, it's worth the trip. When we visited, we got a great deal on Carter sleepers and all-cotton PJs. Leave the credit cards at home. They take only cash or check.

Richie's Children's Shoe
183 Avenue B between 11th and 12th Streets
228-5442

Although customers flock here to get about thirty percent off retail prices on some of the better brands of toddler shoes, they also come to see Richie. A family business for eighty-six years where Richie himself has served the public for fifty of them, this is a class act. Richie is an expert fitter and he will never, ever push you to buy anything. Ask for what you want, as the designer shoes are not always displayed.

Daffy's
111 Fifth Avenue at 18th Street
529-4477
335 Madison Avenue at 44th Street
557-4422
135 East 57th Street between Lexington and
Park Avenues
376-4477
1311 Broadway at 34th Street
736-4477

Daffy's children's department is a great place to find high-quality European and domestic brands at a big discount. However, you need to sort through a ton of junk to find clothing for the appropriate size, sex, and season. It can be a hassle, but if you have the time and the patience, your child will look like a million for at least forty percent less.

Wings for Kids
1519 Third Avenue between 85th and 86th Streets
879-2165

You are sure to find a good buy on practical purchases like PJs (all-cotton), socks, T-shirts, jeans, outerwear, and sneakers. However, whatever you save inside may be spent feeding quarters to the electric car ride out front.

Morris Brothers
2322 Broadway at 84th Street
724-9000

Morris Brothers runs the gamut on all levels. From newborn to teenage sizes, from schlock to excellent quality, and from umbrellas to underwear, you can find it all here at ten to twenty percent off retail.

Old Navy
610 Sixth Avenue at 18th Street
645-0663

Old Navy is a wonderfully cavernous spot for reasonably priced children's clothing. Owned by The Gap, Old Navy's clothing will seem surprisingly familiar but with lower price tags. At Old Navy you can either fully wardrobe your child with style or fill in the "gaps" with things like jeans and one hundred percent cotton turtlenecks. And don't forget to do some shopping of your own here. Top off the day with a cup of joe for you and a glass of milk for him at the coffee shop on the second floor.

Shhh . . . Truly Special Finds

We almost didn't want to tell you. But what we can tell you is that though they may be pricey, they are always precious.

Turtle Dreams
189 Franklin Street between Hudson and Greenwich
Streets
226-1720

An entirely French store carrying clothing designers such as Maria Francesca and Côte Sud. Even their children's books are in French. Bring lots of money so that you can bring home an exquisite outfit for your special tot.

Tvilling
228 Columbus Avenue between 70th and
71st Streets
787-7066

This colorful collection of cotton tee-shirts, dresses, rompers, and leggings (with the cutest matching hats) is adorable and, best of all, affordable. Swedish designer, Vivianne Tvilling, frequently replenishes this tiny store with her hip and fun clothing. Aside from the cotton stuff she also has seasonal prints and velvets.

Tartine et Choclate
746 Madison Avenue between 64th and
65th Streets
744-0975

Perfectly turned-out outfits and oh-so-very French. This store carries extraordinary clothing and accessories for your baby's every need. They even sell their own special pram to transport your babe around in style. Only buy gifts here for your very closest friends and those family members you really like. Price cannot be an object.

Koh's Kids
311 Greenwich Street between Chambers and Reade Streets
791-6915

They say little ones do not need shoes before they can walk. Obviously, they have never been here. From mini cowboy boots to leather slippers adorned with bees, this store has wonderfully imaginative booties to complement any baby fashion statement. They also have tons of tights and socks to maintain the statement once your tot gives the bootie the boot. Aside from cute and trendy clothes, Koh's also designs her own handknit sweaters and dresses.

The Chocolate Soup
946 Madison Avenue between 74th and 75th Streets
861-2210

Bins and bins and bins of beautiful hand-knit sweaters. They also carry hand-painted dresses and other one-of-a-kind pieces. Assorted toys, barrettes, and jewelry round out the store's selection.

Bonne Nuit
30 Lincoln Plaza at Broadway between 62nd and 63rd Streets
262-7740

Here you will find breathtaking children's clothing, layette items, receiving blankets, and hand-knit sweaters and hats by Amy Baht. Come here for all of your very special gift-giving needs. Send anyone who wants to buy something fabulous for your own kids. There are also sexy studs for you (as if . . .).

April Cornell
860 Lexington Avenue between 64th and
65th Streets
570-2775
487 Columbus Avenue between 83rd and
84th Streets
799-4342

Thank heaven for little girls . . . because there's nothing for little boys here. This boutique has wonderfully feminine dresses for both moms and daughters. The flowing floral dresses and hats to accessorize will have you scouring the wedding announcements to find a good garden variety to crash.

Lilliput
265 Lafayette Street between Prince and Spring
Streets
965-9567

There's nothing standard about the "wears" here. Jam-packed with high-end French and American designers, this is a must-shop for those on a chic search. Your child can be styled from head to toe with Lilliput's unique hats, shoes, sweaters, and carefully selected outfits. If you don't feel hosed by the prices, drop by the New York Firefighter's Friend store next door.

Solid Citizens
One-stop shopping. Come here for everything from layettes to toddler wear. You'll find yourself shopping in these stores again and again and again.

Lester's
1522 Second Avenue at 79th Street
734-9292

Lester's has a tremendous selection of European and trendy
clothing (with everything from socks to snowsuits). Their
sales are great, especially midseason. They also carry a full
cruise wear line for warm weather winter vacations. It's
very kid-friendly with a chest full of toys, free balloons, and
a ride on a horse (so bring quarters). They also carry lots
of great shoes (the shoe salesmen are among the best—
they truly know how to fit baby and toddler's shoes) and
layette items can be found at relatively low prices.

Saks Fifth Avenue
611 Fifth Avenue between 49th and 50th Streets
753-4000

A massive children's section committed to providing everything your child could possibly need from birth on. They
are happy to help you register for your layette—a great
thing to do before your baby shower, especially if your
friends and family have suspect taste. Come here for sleepers, bibs, hooded towel sets, and gorgeous sweater outfits,
not to mention scads of beautiful clothing.

Gap Kids
60 West 34th Street near 6th Avenue (biggest in the
world)
643-8995

Walk out your door. Strap on your baby. Walk ten blocks
and you're bound to run into a Gap Kids. With twelve locations and counting, Gap Kids has proliferated throughout
the city. It is an excellent source for good basics for both
boys and girls. If you're looking for jeans, T-shirts, socks,
and other basics with a twist, look no further. Many stores

now have bedding too. Gap Kids in Herald Square is huge. In fact, it's the largest in the world.

One Note Wonders

There are actually some things you do *have* to buy. When you're on a mission to find things like outerwear, bathing suits, or layette items, it's helpful to know of at least one great place you can count on. These stores are great for other things too, but are particularly noteworthy for these specific items.

Z'Baby Company
100 West 72nd Street at Columbus Avenue
579-2229

This upscale, upper West Side boutique offers the finest in trendy and pricey layette items and bedding. The salespeople will help you choose a layette for both a boy and girl. Then, after you give birth, just call and let them know what sex the baby is. They will tactfully show your friends the stuff you chose.

Small Change
964 Lexington Avenue between 70th and
71st Streets
772-6455

The largest selection of outerwear we have ever seen. When we visited, half the store was devoted to coats, jackets, and snowsuits. If you can't find it here, it wasn't made. For those of you with swimming on your mind, this store has a great selection of bathing suits with swimmies built in. (Not easy to find.)

Baby Palace
1410 Lexington Avenue between 92nd and
93rd Streets
426-4544

A recent scramble to find swim diapers brought us here.
Were we pleased! Swim diapers galore with tropical sea-
horses and starfish to boot. This is also a paraphernalia
palace (see Chapter 2).

Bloomingdale's
1000 Third Avenue between 59th and 60th Streets
705-2000 (general)
705-2670 (infant department)

With so much to choose from, the seventh floor cannot be
ignored for layette items and basic clothing needs. Watch
for sales (they always seem to occur two days after your
visit). The salespeople are very helpful for first time layet-
tees.

Little Feet
If the shoe fits, they'll wear it. It is essential to go to a place
with an experienced and patient fitter. With a good fitter, even the
shyest child can be coaxed into stepping onto the Ritz stick long
enough for proper measurement. For summer sandals, buy early
because, like the city's population, there's virtually none left by mid-
June.

Little Eric Shoes
133B Third Avenue at 76th Street
288-8987
1118 Madison Avenue at 83rd Street
717-1513

Imelda may have started young with a visit to this Upper
East Side shoe salon. The large selection of stylish and

trendy shoes, sneakers, and boots will bring out the fetishist in just about anyone. The salespeople are patient and well able to properly fit even the squirmiest little feet. Remember to bring quarters for the horsey ride.

Shoofly
465 Amsterdam Avenue between 82nd and 83rd Streets
580-4390
42 Hudson Street between Duane and Thomas Streets
406-3270

If chic feet are what you're after and you are willing to pay for them, Shoofly is the place. Their tremendous selection of fine European brands establishes them as trendsetters for tots. The selection of basic walking shoes and sneakers is somewhat limited. The salespeople are kind, patient, know how to fit a shoe, and don't push. At Shoofly, they don't bother you. Also noteworthy are the accessories (hats, socks, hair stuff).

East Side Kids
1298 Madison Avenue at 92nd Street
360-5000

Mom always said, "Make sure you have on practical shoes!" Well, she'd be pleased with this selection of footwear that is practical and classic (with names like Start-rite and Sonnet). The prices can also be more practical than some other uptown shops, and the big sale rack can make for some opportunistic shopping. Bring your child's old shoes with you and drop them in the bin in back—East Side Kids donates them to charity.

Harry's Shoes
2299 Broadway at 83rd Street
874-2035

For your child's first pair of shoes, there's no place like
Harry's. They carry all the basics like Stride Rite, Jumping
Jacks, and Elefanten. While the wait can be long, the experienced, gentle fitting is well worth it. Besides pulling all
of the socks off the wall display, your child won't find much
to do, so bring some toys.

CHAPTER 9

Food and Whine

RESTAURANTS

Although your reservations will change from two at the corner table to two and a high chair, New York can still be the dining capital of the world for you and your family. Your four star criteria, however, will change from food, decor, service, and atmosphere to fun, fast, and family-friendly.

While there are literally thousands of restaurants in New York, not all of them are ready, willing, and able to weather your child's fledgling table manners. We've listed our favorites (not always based on food) throughout the city, from those fundamentally focused on children to your old haunts that won't shut you out merely because you're now a proud parent.

Wee Are Family

These restaurants provide a relatively stress-free family eating experience. You never have to feel self-conscious here; from finding space for your oversized carriage to weathering your two-year-old's temper tantrums, they're family-friendly. While you may not run into Julia Child, they offer a broad range of acceptably edible cuisine.

Tony's Di Napoli
1606 Second Avenue between 83rd and
84th Streets
861-8686

If your party can agree on an entree or two, this family style restaurant is a solid choice. The big portions of pasta, salad, or chicken can satisfy both parents and children alike. They also do not seem to mind the big portions of pasta, salad, or chicken that end up on the floor underneath the high chair.

Lenge
1465 Third Avenue between 83rd and
82nd Streets
535-9661
200 Columbus Avenue at 69th Street
799-9188

Dinner in one of their Ume rooms is a real treat for any New Yorker for whom the dining room is the living room is the playroom. While you enjoy some good sushi, tempura, or teriyaki, your children can spill, cry, or eat in the privacy of your own little room. Just make sure everyone has on clean socks.

America
9 East 18th Street between Broadway and
Fifth Avenue
505-2110

Kid-friendly is an understatement during weekend brunch time. The bar area is converted into a play area and the waiters, attitudinally speaking, become preschool teach-ers. You'll get a balloon sculpture before you've had a chance to read the novel-like menu. The food is plentiful and includes many of your childhood favorites (such as fluffernutter sandwiches and mini burgers topped with Velveeta).

Dallas B-B-Que
1265 Third Avenue between 72nd and 73rd Streets
772-9393
27 West 72nd Street between Central Park West and Columbus Avenue
873-2004
21 University Place at 8th Street
674-4450
132 Second Avenue at St. Marks Place
777-5574

Yippee yi yeah! The fixin's here are plentiful and the restaurant is spacious. Stick with the ribs or chicken and get fries and cornbread to go with it. Drinks are so big three kids can share one soda . . . in theory anyway. Whether you choose to sit in their faux greenhouse or anywhere inside, don't worry about the kids ruining your neighbor's meal. Why? A good attitude is a prerequisite for dining here.

Ollie's
2957 Broadway at 116th Street
932-3300
2315 Broadway at 84th Street
362-3712
200 West 44th Street between Broadway and Eighth Avenue
921-5988

Despite the crowds and the cafeteria-like atmosphere, Ollie's is in no way the McDonald's of Chinese food. On the contrary, the food is always delicious, fresh, and nutritious. The vast assortment of steamed and fresh food including fish, vegetables, and dumplings make for a more interesting way to have your child experience at least some of the requisite food groups.

Carmine's
2450 Broadway between 90th and 91st Streets
362-2200
200 West 44th Street between Broadway and
8th Avenue
221-3800

Just follow the scent of garlic to these popular family-style Italian restaurants. The food is delicious and the portions are immense, but so are the waits (up to two hours on Friday and Saturday nights). They do take and honor reservations for large parties, so invite your in-laws, neighbors, friends and co-workers . . . you'll only need to order two dishes to feed them all! Take-out is also a great option.

Luke's Bar & Grill
1394 Third Avenue between 79th and 80th Streets
249-7070

For brunch, lunch, or dinner, the burgers and fries are among the city's best. The dining room is frequently filled with children enjoying grilled cheese and friendly service. While they do not have a children's menu, you can create a cost-effective meal by sharing a big juicy burger with your little one.

20 Mott Street
20 Mott Street between Pell Street and
Chatham Square
964-0380

Just getting there can be an adventure, so it's a good thing that the name and the address are one and the same. With Peking ducks hanging in storefront windows and tanks of eels, Chinatown can be an eye-opening experience for children. The great fresh food, fish tank, and friendly service make 20 Mott Street one of the best the area has to offer.

EJ's Luncheonette
1271 Third Avenue at 73rd Street
472-0600
447 Amsterdam Avenue between 81st and
82nd Streets
873-3444
432 Sixth Avenue between 9th and 10th Streets
473-5555

This is a perfect case in which kids change your opinion of a restaurant. For breakfast, lunch, or dinner, it satisfies the three tenets of dining with kids—fast, fun, and friendly. All of your family favorites can be found here; burgers, pancakes, grilled cheese, and fries. Don't arrive with a sleeping infant as there is no room for strollers at tableside.

Brother Jimmy's
1461 First Avenue at 76th Street
288-0999
1644 Third Avenue at 92nd Street
426-2020

Who says there's no such thing as a free lunch . . . or dinner? At Brother Jimmy's, the kids eat free (with a dining adult, of course). With choices like chicken fingers, burgers, and fries, most children will actually eat their dinner. It's pretty noisy, but the bar music will either send your tots off to bop or drown out the shrieks . . . of delight, that is.

Pongsri Thai
106 Bayard Street at Baxter Street
349-3132

Don't be alarmed by the somewhat grungy appearance.
Pongsri Thai is clean, inexpensive, and child-friendly. And,
most importantly, the authentic Thai food is extraordinary
and surprisingly tasty to a child's palate. If you love the food
here, check out their other locations, too.

Pipeline
2 World Financial Center
225 Liberty Street
945-2755

If you can weather the whipping winter winds, a weekend
dinner here is a must. This restaurant sets up a play area
complete with videos for your tots to wander off to before,
during, or after the meal and offers kids meals for only $1.95
(with purchase of a grown-up meal). The cute kiddy menu,
which doubles as a clown mask, has the standard fare but
the prices are a little high. So, it pays for you to down a
burger too.

Not at Your Home Cooking

Let's face it, many New York parents are secretly psyched that
their tiny kitchens aren't conducive to simmering stews and baking
brownies. No matter, there are endless options to go out for at-
home cooking in a nice, relaxed environment.

Sarabeth's
1295 Madison Avenue between 92nd and
93rd Streets
410-7335
423 Amsterdam Avenue between 80th and
81st Streets
496-6280

This is perhaps the only instance in which you will be thankful that your children are up before the sun on the weekends. If you can beat the crowd, you will enjoy a relaxing and delicious brunch. From pancakes to omelets to fresh muffins to cereal, the meal is certain to please. Remember that there is always the option of an early afternoon nap for the whole family.

Friend of a Farmer
77 Irving Place between 18th and 19th Streets
477-2188

Not quite Old MacDonald's, this old country setting can help set the tone though not guarantee a relaxing meal. The child-friendly environment, complete with children's menu and cheerful wait staff, seems to be an anomaly in Gramercy Park. The service can be a little slow—but don't worry, just grab a banana off the windowsill.

Main Street
446 Columbus Avenue between 81st and
82nd Streets
873-5025

This is the quintessential family restaurant with delicious home cooking. Everything about it from the meat loaf and macaroni to the wide aisles for sleeping babies in strollers to the friendly service screams "kids welcome here." It's quite acceptable for your kids to scream, too.

Good Enough to Eat
483 Amsterdam Avenue between 83rd and
84th Streets
496-0163

It's warm, cozy, and tasty. With hot cinnamonny French toast and big glasses of cold chocolate milk for kids, big crunchy salads for moms (or vice versa), and great desserts for all—it's a wonderful experience for the whole family. Don't go when your tot is tired or especially hungry, because the wait can be long.

E.A.T.
1064 Madison Avenue between 80th and 81st
Streets
772-0022

The place to see and be seen. Their menu has something to please any tot, even mom's meat loaf sandwiches. Also good to know is that you almost can't find another place in New York City to spend more money—now that's saying something.

Popover Café
551 Amsterdam Avenue between 86th and 87th
Streets
595-8555

Popover Café is a comfortable, child-friendly place—complete with teddy bears, high chairs, and charming, patient staff. The kids love the popovers and French toast. While salads are available, parents love the popovers and French toast, too. Best known for brunch, with kids it is actually a much better choice for a late lunch or dinner as waiting is uncommon after 2 P.M.

Bubby's
120 Hudson Street between Franklin and North
Moore Streets
219-0666

Home cooking at its best, Bubby's is the quintessential
kids spot for TriBeCa brunchers. While there is no official
kid's menu, the friendly and helpful wait staff will serve
one pancake or one piece of French toast to your little
one. As this is one of the few kid-friendly places in an
area of town filled with chic spots, go at off-hours or be
prepared to wait.

Sugar and Spice, Try Not to Think Twice

One of the many benefits of having a child is having an excuse
to add 10,000 calories to your daily count. Just remember, if you
didn't actually order it for yourself, you're allowed to discount the
calories by seventy percent. These places have unbelievable treats
for especially deserving tots . . . and parents.

Serendipity
225 East 60th Street between Second and Third
Avenues
838-3531

Unbelievably long hot dogs, burgers, grilled cheese, and
desserts beyond your wildest dreams. A famous frozen hot
chocolate can easily feed a family of four . . . teen. However, if your child should serendipitously wander from the
table, beware, for they are not fans of kids in the way. Also
keep your eyes on the toys for sale right when you walk in
the door.

Peppermint Park Café
1225 First Avenue near 66th Street
288-5054

The peppermint candy–striped awnings outside get you in
the mood for what's inside. With a dining room as big as a
suburban Friendly's, this is the perfect place for a clandestine banana split breakdown. Peppermint Park makes all its
own ice cream, and they also stock tons of candy.

Piu Bello
2152 Broadway between 75th and 76th Streets
799-0011

Gallons of gelato, showboats of sorbets, and plenty of pas-
tries ... in this establishment you'll find something for
everyone. It's very spacious—bring the whole family. There
are fat-free fruit flavors and lots of decadent stuff too.

Rumpelmayer's
50 Central Park South at Sixth Avenue
located in St. Moritz Hotel
446-5525

Heavenly hot chocolate served in proper china pots with
accompanying china mugs—splendid! The wait for a table
can sometimes be trying, but at least it's not out in the cold.
You can spend it hanging out in the lobby of the St. Moritz
Hotel. Service is not always up to snuff but the desserts
surely are. Famously festive around the holidays, this is the
place to come after a skate at Wollman Rink.

Ciao Bella
27 East 92nd Street between Madison and Fifth
Avenues
831-5555

With so many decadent flavors of gelato like malted milk
ball and hazelnut biscotti to choose from, you won't even
consider the regular ice cream. On a warm afternoon, it is
the perfect pit stop after a romp in the park or a stroll down
Madison. Lots of parents can't resist trying to sneak a big
lick of their child's cone.

Moon Dog Brand Ice Cream
378 Bleecker Street between Perry and Charles
Streets
675-4540

Ice cream and apple pie, the fundamental dessert in the
good old American diet. Tucked away in the West Village,
this charming treat spot has unbelievable ice cream, little
pies, and huge Rice Krispies treats. The only lowfat option
is sorbet. Your child is sure to have worked up an appetite
for this at the Bleecker Playground down the street.

Emack & Bolio's
389 Amsterdam Avenue between 78th and
79th Streets
362-2747

As much for you as for your tot, this decadent yet healthy
shop comes straight to New York City from Boston. You
won't believe there are fat-free yogurt flavors like Snickers
and Milky Way. For the really skeptical, they list fat grams
and calories in full view. They also have fruit and vegetable
drinks.

CBK of New York Cookies
226 East 83rd Street between Second and
Third Avenues
794-3383
336 Amsterdam Avenue between 77th and
78th Streets
787-7702

Aside from birthday baked goods, these stores have plenty of "if you finish your dinner, you can have one of these" treats. Check out the bear-shaped Rice Krispies treats, mini cupcakes, and jars of penny candy (for lots more than a penny).

Pug Bros. Popcorn
565 Columbus between 72nd and 73rd Streets
595-4780

Just because you don't get out to the movies anymore doesn't mean you can't experience some great popcorn. While the selection is limited, the swiss chocolate, caramel, and melted cheddar flavors are unsurpassed.

Pommes Frites
123 Second Avenue between 7th and 8th Streets
674-1234

Okay, so it isn't sugar or spice, but it is oh-so-decadent. As the name would lead you to believe, french fries are the only fare at this East Village take-out. In sizes that range from giant to humungous and flavors that range from tasty to scrumptious, this is sure to be a remarkable treat for kids of any size.

Surprise . . . Party of Three

Don your preparental attitude and save yourself the babysitting fee. Surprise, kids *are* welcome at some pretty cool spots.

Mesa City
1059 Third Avenue between 62nd and 63rd Streets
207-1919

Once upon a time, Bobby Flay had a little baby named Sophie, and these days even the manager of this restaurant has a little one! All of this makes for a fabulous family eating experience complete with plain cheese quesadillas served promptly to your little ones.

White Horse Tavern
567 Hudson Street at 11th Street
989-3956

Oh, the memories! In better weather, it's best to sit outside at their picnic tables (not much smoke) and fantastic people watching—especially on Halloween (all those creative costumes). The chili can't be beat, and you can count on burgers and stuff for the younger ones and a great selection of beer for you. Remember not to drink and stroll.

Empire Diner
210 Tenth Avenue at 22nd Street
243-2736

A sophisticated take on your basic diner, the food is quite good and the hot chocolate is better. Everything is fresh, even their orange juice (you'll think you're in Florida). Don't be put off by the familiar silver-bullet exterior; inside the atmosphere is exceedingly pleasant and they even have a piano player.

NoHo Star
330 Lafayette Street at Bleecker Street
925-0070

Here's a perfect case in which a child will *not* change your opinion of a restaurant. The eclectic menu (mandarin chicken to meat loaf) offers options equally delicious for parent and child. It is also a fun spot for celebrity sighting (you can see your favorite stars wiping drool off their children's chins). Except for weekend brunches, the wait is minimal.

Aggie's
146 West Houston Street at MacDougal Street
673-8994

Primarily known for its delicious, reasonably priced brunches and long lines, Aggie's is a great off-hours spot for kids. Whether you live in the neighborhood or are looking for a cool respite, Aggie's is a good choice for delicious burgers and salads.

Palm
873 Second Avenue between 44th and 45th Streets
687-2953
Palm Too
840 Second Avenue between 44th and 45th Streets
697-5198

On the rare occasion when money is not an issue and you are dying for something rare and juicy, this can be a treat. If you go early, sit in a spacious booth upstairs, and order quickly, it can actually be a comfortable experience. To defray the cost, let your child eat off your plate or order some chicken nuggets and enjoy them for the next three days.

Louie's West Side Cafe
441 Amsterdam between 81st and 82nd Streets
877-1900

Brunch here is the way it used to be. Quiet. Bloody Mary's.
Mimosas. Great omelets with grown-up ingredients. A great
table up front next to the picture windows. But don't forget
your child's sunglasses, squinting over waffles can ruin a
meal.

Mayrose
920 Broadway between 21st and 22nd Streets
533-3663

You may be tempted by the display of home-cooked desserts as you enter. But one glance at the menu and you will
want to eat a real meal first. You are going to love the big
windows, natural light, and people-watching. And with hot
dogs, fries, and fresh-off-the-farm glass-bottled chocolate
milk, your kids will be crying . . . for more.

Odeon
145 West Broadway at Thomas Street
233-0507

Ten years ago you were the last to leave this incredibly cool
bar scene. Now you can be the first one in to enjoy the sassy
seats, the bright blue ginger ale, the kiddy menu, and . . .
the delicious bistro menu.

Arqua
281 Church Street at White Street
334-1888

If you bring your own sassy seat, your children will be able
to tell grandma you took them to Italy. Seriously, it does

feel like Tuscany. The food is phenomenal, the atmosphere is alluring, and you'll feel comfortable having kids here. You may even begin to feel romantic until you remember it's time to cut the penne into bite-sized pieces.

Florent Restaurant
69 Gansevoort Street between Greenwich and
Washington Streets
989-5779

So it's 3:00 A.M., your child's up, and you're hungry. Only in New York can you hit a truly cool spot in the wee hours. Complete with excellent bistro fare, children's menu, and neighborhood transvestites, Florent can make endless nights with children something you can actually look forward to. They're open twenty-four hours!

Spring Street Natural
62 Spring Street at Lafayette Street
966-0290

Child-friendly service is an understatement here. From offering to make room at the table for a big stroller to producing a balloon (really a surgical glove) with the check, they make you feel as though they're actually glad you brought a baby. The menu is full of wonderfully healthy foods, like sandwiches, salads, soup, eggs, and *fries*, of course.

Petaluma
1356 First Avenue at 73rd Street
772-8800

Petaluma is a rare combination of truly delicious adult fare and truly child-friendly service. While mom is dining on a plate of fabulous fusilli, the kids can watch (and occasionally participate in) the preparation of brick oven pizza (the ovens are in plain sight). Outside seating in warmer weather is also available.

Cub Room Café
183 Prince Street at Sullivan Street
777-0030

A completely unexpected surprise! After a day's stroll, it's great to stop here for an early dinner. They have no kid's menu but almost everything for grown-ups can be modified for children. An eclectic menu ranging from burgers to omelettes to lamb chops makes it a tasty treat for the whole family.

Pizza Face
Save Pizza Hut for your next trip out of town. On this city's superhighway of food, you could eat pizza every night for the next twenty years and never have the same thing twice. OK, so maybe we're exaggerating just a little.

John's Pizzeria
408 East 64th Street between First and
York Avenues
935-2895
48 West 65th Street between Columbus Avenue and
Central Park West
721-7001
278 Bleecker Street between Sixth and
Seventh Avenues
243-1680

If you're tired of Ray's, Original Ray's, Definitely Ray's, This Ray's, and so on, visit one of John's locations. Here your family can enjoy great brick oven pizza that in no way resembles any relative of Ray's. The line can be quite long, so venture out a little before your desired mealtime.

Sofia's Fabulous Pizza
1022 Madison Avenue at 79th Street
734-2676

Head for the top floor, which feels like a giant greenhouse. The staff is incredibly accommodating to your children (even to a nine-month-old). They serve half portions of adult food and the noise level is comfortably high.

Two Boots
37 Avenue A between 2nd and 3rd Streets
505-2276

You know they *know* kids when the crayons and paper are in place before you've taken your seats. Between the cute pizza face (big enough to feed two children and/or a parent) and the Planters Punk juice, your child is sure to enjoy the meal. A big plus is the large, clean bathroom with lots of space to change a diaper.

Pizzeria Uno
220 East 86th Street between Second and
Third Avenues
472-5656
432 Columbus Avenue at 81st Street
595-4700
55 Third Avenue between 10th and 11th Streets
995-9668
391 Sixth Avenue between 8th Street and
Waverly Place
242-5230
89 South Street at the South Street Seaport
791-7999

A kiddy menu, cups with tops, and crayon-ready tables . . . what more can you ask for? *Really good food.* You can't always have everything.

Pintaile's Pizza
26 East 91st Street between Madison and
Fifth Avenues
722-1967
1443 York Avenue between 76th and 77th Streets
717-4990

A favorite snack spot for nearby students, this tiny place seats about six people (not counting the two benches outside). But don't be put off, the pizza is superb. Their menu sports gourmet twists on old standbys; try goat cheese and sun-dried tomatoes and pick the toppings off your child's slice.

California Pizza Kitchen
201 East 60th Street at Third Avenue
755-7773

You cannot dream up a pizza that this restaurant cannot make. Because this restaurant is as big as the state of California, if you are meeting another family here, pick a specific meeting spot. (Or else you'll spend that ever-so-small window of opportunity when your children are geared up to eat in search of your friends.)

Patsy's Pizza
2287 First Avenue between 117th and
118th Streets
534-9783
61 West 74th Street between Columbus Avenue and
Central Park West
579-3000
509 Third Avenue between 34th and 35th Streets
689-7500

On the West Side, go directly to the back room. Here, you won't feel self-conscious if your child's the one tossing the dough in the air. The brick oven pizza is delicious but if you're trying to lose a few, the salads are great, too. Not the usual pizza parlor fare, they are plentiful and exotic. Make your mind up quickly because it takes a while to get your food.

CHAPTER 10

Here Comes the Bribe

TOY STORES

Inevitably, parents spend more time and money than they would like to in toy stores (and in this case time is money). Between birthday parties and bribe toys (yes, we all do it), one can expect to visit a shop at least three times a month. But the joy of every child does not have to be the nightmare of every parent if you know the best place to go to find what you need.

Upper East Side

Noodle Kidoodle
112 East 86th Street between Lexington and
Park Avenues
427-6611

Substreet level but not substandard, this store is good for gifts (especially around the holidays) as all age groups are well represented. Most noteworthy is the selection of science stuff, computer software, and crafts. While you shop, your children can play with the Brio train set up in the middle of the store or try the latest computer games at the terminals. Prices are good for the top brands. Excellent wrapping and daily local East Side delivery are available.

A Bear's Place
789 Lexington Avenue between 61st and
62nd Streets
826-6465

Not only the big selection of Battat toys, but plenty of other beautiful stuff will make your child want to hibernate in his room. Here, even the ordinary is extraordinary. For example, instead of the typical plastic kitchen, they have hand-painted wooden stoves that would look great next to any Sub-Zero appliance. In addition to one or two Barbies, they have collectible dolls and hand-painted shelves on which to display them. They also have beautiful hand-painted furniture and comfy little chintz couches.

Hom Boms
A Toy and Craft Emporium
1500 First Avenue between 78th and 79th Streets
717-5300

This relatively small space is chock-a-block with everything a growing child wants. The store caters to infants through elementary school age children, and has the largest selection we've seen of Thomas the Tank Engine and Playmobile toys. They also have an extensive cache of Mustela products including that hard-to-find sunblock stick. A sign on their shelves proclaims that they will meet or beat any Upper East Side competitor's prices (between 59th and 96th Streets). They also host sand art and T-shirt art projects in their back room for up to six children at a time (age three and over). Call the store for project times and prices.

Ben's for Kids
1380 Third Avenue between 78th and 79th Streets
794-2330

Ben's is a great neighborhood store. Prices tend to be on the high side, but the selection of infant/toddler gifts is good. Along with popular brands like Tonka, Little Tykes, Fisher Price, and Crayola, they have a small but good selection of books, videos, audio cassettes, bikes, and sleds. It's also easy to shop with tots as the fish tank is quite mesmerizing.

Mary Arnold Toys
962 Lexington Avenue between 70th and
71st Streets
744-8510

This store is jam-packed with lots of everything . . . board games, infant toys, puzzles, crafts, and so on. In addition, they have the increasingly harder to find matchbox cars, action figures, and Barbie dolls, which seem to have been knocked from the inventory of more *educationally* oriented stores. Daily delivery is available.

Bear Hugs & Baby Dolls, Inc.
311 East 81st Street between First and
Second Avenues
717-1514

Nestled on a quiet tree-lined street, this tiny store is brimming with bears, bears, and more bears. Claiming to be New York City's "Muffy VanderBear" headquarters, they have in stock every possible outfit for Muffy from cruise wear to holiday costumes. They will even custom order your child's school uniform in Muffy's size. Bear Hugs also has a concentrated array of Pooh paraphernalia and stocks Madame Alexander dolls.

Upper West Side

Little Extras
550 Amsterdam between 86th and 87th Sts
721-6161

You won't find one piece of extruded plastic here. This shop offers unique and personalized toys and gifts for special occasions. Popular items include measuring sticks and hand-painted stools for the bathroom bound toddler. Even educational toys are unique and more fun than usual, like whistling shape sorters and wooden puzzles. Be warned, prices are high and the salespeople are persuasive. We don't recommend it for a quickie bribe toy.

Penny Whistle Toys
448 Columbus Avenue at 81st Street
873-9090
1283 Madison Avenue between 91st and
92nd Streets
369-3868

You can't miss the bubbles wafting on Columbus Avenue. Perfect for quick treats, these stores have a good selection of inexpensive trinkets that offer your child a great diversion as you shop for big-ticket items. To the average three-year-old, a rubber frog for $3.50 can be a lot more interesting than the $50 Radio Flyer you may be pining for. Also, the West Side store has a room with action figures hidden in the back.

My Favorite Place
265 West 87th Street between Broadway and
West End Avenue
362-5320

Be sure to have your favorite credit card in hand at this haven for the gotta-have-its. Their toy selection is particularly well-suited to the under-three crew as they have Brio, Crayola crafts, Little Tykes, Playmobile, and Fisher Price. Last minute shoppers can pick up a great gift before heading to the birthday party rooms housed in this shop.

Uncle Futz
408 Amsterdam at 79th Street
799-6723

For those who do not like to futz around, Uncle Futz is a great store. Their well-chosen, relatively small selection of toys, books, and gift items makes it easy to shop for kids of all ages. The educational toys are gifts that will make both children and parents happy. Also worth noting are the personalized items ranging from stationery to stools. Local neighborhood delivery is free.

West Side Kids
498 Amsterdam at 84th Street
496-7282

This store provides idiot-proof shopping for those who question their ability to select age-appropriate toys. The store is organized by age group and the salespeople are extremely helpful about suggesting the right toy. They have a moderate selection of quality items including Brio trains, stuffed animals, and musical instruments. They also do lovely gift wrapping. They only deliver within five blocks and charge $5. One watch-out: The open containers of tiny toys can be lifted by your tiny tots (by the age of two, most kids have accidently shoplifted at least once).

Midtown

Toys 'R Us
1293 Broadway at 34th Street
594-8697
24-32 Union Square East between 15th and
16th Streets
674-8697

This store makes you realize that the prices at F. A. O.
Schwarz definitely reflect their real estate. It's big like the
suburbs, cheap like the suburbs, and nothing special like
the suburbs. But you can't ignore Toys 'R Us, where toys
can be found for a lot less. Also, it's great for holiday bulk
shopping and for big items like bikes and ride-on toys.

Second Star to the Right
437 Third Avenue between 30th and 31st Streets
679-0006

You name it, a name is on it. In addition to toys, they carry
a wide variety of personalized gifts including mobiles and
wall hangings. Barbie and Brio also make an appearance
here.

Wynken, Blynken & Nod's
306 East 55th Street between First and Second
Avenues
308-9299

The mix of precious antiques (a wooden Pinocchio figurine
and a full-size carousel horse, for example) and innovative
new toys make this one of the more imaginative stores
around. Beyond the toys and accessories, this boutique also
has beautiful clothing, both new and antique. Whether you
end up buying something old or something new here, you
will not want it to end up as something borrowed.

TriBeCa/Village

Kidding Around
60 West 15th Street between Fifth and
Sixth Avenues
645-6337
68 Bleecker Street between Broadway and Lafayette
Streets
598-0228

This store carries just about everything, although you have to look up, down and all around to see it all. From big items such as Kettler bikes and Italian-made play washing machine/laundry centers to puzzles, balls, games, and lots of little trinkets (making it perfect for a quickie), you'll be certain to find a wonderful and imaginative gift. They also have a big selection of puppets, puzzles, and unique dolls and accessories.

Just Jakes
40 Hudson Street between Duane and
Thomas Streets
267-1716

For those in search of creative gifts, Just Jakes is just right. Along with wooden dollhouses, unique instruments (including a little steel drum), and innovative baby toys, they have a lot of craft items. Keep an eye out for the extensive selection of paints, rubber stamps, and great storage cases to keep your budding artist's studio well organized.

Tootsies
543 Hudson Street between Perry and
Charles Streets
242-0182

Great for the under-three set, Tootsies is a lovely little shop
for lots of little things. Noteworthy are the accessories for
all of your child's favorite books such as Spot, Peter Rabbit,
and Curious George. They also have a nice selection of
wooden puzzles, toys, and great soft books.

Quest Toys
225 Liberty Street (Two World Financial Center)
945-9330

Even if you don't live in Battery Park City, this is a great
find for those working in the financial district. Don't be de-
ceived by the small size of this store. Inside, you'll find an
ample supply of educational toys, puzzles, balls, stuffed animals, and art supplies. Don't forget to look up and check
out the marionettes hanging from the ceiling.

CHAPTER 11

Literary Playgrounds

BOOKSTORES

Reading to your child doesn't necessarily mean cuddling on the sofa anymore. In New York, it can mean bundling up and going out to your favorite bookstore. More and more, bookstores have become gathering places where children can explore the literary world and bump into their playmates, all without having to be quiet and still. These bookstores also offer author readings, which just might rival your best rendition of *Are You My Mother?* Also, don't forget your local public library—it's a great resource.

Upper East Side

Barnes and Noble, Jr.
120 East 86th Street between Lexington and
Park Avenues
427-0686

Reading time isn't quiet time here. These stores are like playgrounds for small children. They can take books off the shelves to read or just to pile on the floor. Each month instructors come from local programs (like the 92nd Street Y) for some organized fun. Staff members perform weekly story time and occasionally, authors read their books aloud to the kids. Check the monthly calendar of events for more details. They also have a limited selection of videos, well-concealed at the check-out counter.

Bookberries
983 Lexington Avenue at 71st Street
794-9400

As inviting for little ones as its name implies. Here, the children's section is like a cozy cave set off from the rest of the store. There's also an adorable child-sized chair for sophisticated readers. Board books are well placed for children and shelves are prominently labeled for parents on the go. The selection of books is well thought out here, and not super-commercial.

Lenox Hill Bookstore
1018 Lexington Avenue between 72nd and 73rd Streets
472-7170

This is a wonderfully charming bookstore, which captures the essence of what reading time should be—relaxing and quiet. The kid's section in the rear of the store is very user-friendly for tiny tots. It has a center island with colorful board books within easy reach for little ones. A bench with two pillows is conveniently located for weary parents. Small warning: A limited selection of stuffed toys (mostly companions to books like Sendak's *Where The Wild Things Are*) are within sight and grab of even the littlest fingers.

Upper West Side

Bank Street Bookstore
610 West 112th Street at Broadway
875-4550

Enter this bookstore and you feel like you have brought
your kids to an intellectual mecca (maybe that's because
Bank Street School owns it). They carry every book imaginable and some you won't find in other stores; for instance,
special needs books about sign language/deafness, home-
lessness, adoption, toilet training, and death. They even
carry poetry books for children. Bank Street does sell some
toys located in the back of the store behind the stairs. Video
and cassette recordings are available for purchase as well.
The staff is incredibly friendly and most helpful.

Gryphon
2246 Broadway between 80th and 81st Streets
362-0706

This is not an outing spot for your children but rather for
you. This store is really, really tiny, but oh, what a gem. If
you are willing to look, you will find all the books you read
as a child—in hardcover. Book series such as The Bobbsey
Twins, Nancy Drew, and The Hardy Boys as well as your
favorite fairy tales line the shelves. For a small amount of
money, you can bring the joy of your childhood to your tiny
tots.

Chelsea/Gramercy Park/Union Square

Barnes & Noble
33 East 17th Street between Park Avenue and
Broadway

If your destination is the Greenmarket at Union Square or
ABC Carpet, make this store a part of your trip. The chil-

dren's section is huge and truly inviting. Miniature Adirondack chairs, benches, and tables are scattered throughout the space, or you can just sprawl on the floor. The walls are sky blue with painted murals of all your child's favorite storybook characters—Pooh, Eloise, Dr. Seuss. Storytelling takes place on a stage every Saturday and a guest author is featured once a month. It goes without saying that the books are plentiful and there is even a restroom with a baby changing station. Top off your excursion with lunch at America around the corner on 18th Street.

Books of Wonder
16 West 18th Street between Fifth and
Sixth Avenues
989-3270

This store, devoted solely to children, is a wonder! It has a great selection of children's favorites in all age categories and especially for little ones. It's the place to come for your entire "book bug" needs. They even have first edition hardcover children's favorites in a special glass cabinet. Books of Wonder offers Sunday morning story time for the two-and-over set and for parents they have a newsletter filled with information on the latest books and a schedule of events.

East/West Village

St. Marks Bookshop
31 Third Avenue near 9th Street
260-7853

This just might be the hippest bookshop in town. Your kids will think they've entered a futuristic world—all the bookshelves are fashioned out of water pipes. The children's section here feels vastly different than at the mega bookstores. It's a lot less commercial and your child won't be bombarded by Barney.

The Strand
828 Broadway near 12th Street
473-1452

A book lover's landmark, The Strand has a huge children's section downstairs. Look for an alphabetical directory and a map of the section at the foot of the stairs. Do bring your three- and-four-year-olds. They will love exploring a real bookstore. Books are displayed from floor to ceiling and everywhere in between. Don't forget to buy something for yourself.

Tootsie's
554 Hudson Street between Perry and 11th Street
242-0182

Toot, toot, tootsie, don't cry because there are tons of books here from wall to wall. You'll find every book you need to coax your child into a budding Jane Austen. A little reading table and chairs welcome those who want to hang. Additional inducements: toys! They hang from the ceiling, they're on the walls, and they're on the shelves. Tootsie's also offers story time on Saturdays at 10:00 A.M. for children ages three and up.

Downtown

The Drawing Center
35 Wooster Street between Grand and
Broome Streets
219-2166

A beautiful stark white gallery, The Drawing Center hosts Nightlight for Kids, organized by Linda Yablonsky. Nightlight presents storytelling by children's authors and other notable people. A past example is the Tony Award–winning playwright Wendy Wasserstein reading *Pamela's First Musical*. These readings are held every other month on Sunday afternoons. The recommended age for children is four and up, but all children are welcome.

Rizzoli Bookstore
3 World Financial Center at Vesey Street and
West Side Highway
945-0505

Located in the Winter Garden, this store has a separate entrance for the children's section and its own cash register for a quick getaway. The store is lined on two sides by wide low shelves perfect for tiny bottoms. The shelves are littered with board books to look at, to hold, and to explore. Once a year, Rizzoli sponsors a fun-filled book fair in the Winter Garden—your kid's favorite characters make guest appearances, authors tell their stories, and children can enjoy face painting and arts & crafts.

SoHo Books
351 West Broad between Broome and
Grand Streets
226-3395

This bookstore has a small children's section right in front tucked near a big window. With opera playing in the background, your child can have a ball pulling books off the shelves. All books are adorned with large neon circles in day-glo colors (green, orange) with the price of the book in large print—how refreshing. The section is a little cluttered, so be prepared to hunt. When we were there, they had a large basket of kids books outside, each for $1.98.

Spring Street Bookstore
169 Spring Street between West Broad
and Thompson Street
219-3033

Definitely a store for parents who know what they want to
buy. There are lots of children's books, but they're not well-
displayed. A few board books are on floor level and the
section is located across from magazines—in case you need
a *Cosmo* break while your child explores. The books are
organized by categories such as preschool, cloth picture
books, educational, and fairy tales.

New York Public Libraries

Office of Children's Services
340-0904 (0903)
Hours: M-F, 9:00 A.M. to 5:00 P.M.

Each of the New York Public Library's satellite branches
offers free organized picture book hour or film programs
for the two- to six-year-old set. Occasionally, they host special programs featuring things like magicians, music and
movement, or animals. And don't forget that as soon as your
child is able to sign his name, he can get his own library
card. Just bring three forms of identification (driver's license, recent phone bill, etc.) to your local branch and
watch your child's eyes light up. If you are uncertain where
your public library is located or desire more information,
call the Office of Children's Services. This is the central
office for all children's branch library programs. Call for the
program schedule for your neighborhood library.

CHAPTER 12

Kiddy Coifs

HAIRCUTS

Whether it's the first, second, or tenth haircut, getting your child coifed can be a laborious and painful process. Choosing a fun environment with patient, experienced stylists can make this a memorable event to which both parent and child can look forward. When choosing a place, it's important to consider how long the wait will be, whether there is a waiting area (especially for siblings in tow), and if there are toys for purchase (these can turn a $22 haircut into a $44 event).

Children's hair salons seem to be an uptown phenomenon so downtowners will need to hop on the bus, which is always fun for the kids.

Cozy's
1125 Madison Avenue between 84th and 85th Streets
744-1716
448 Amsterdam Avenue between 80th and 81st
Streets
579-2600

Cozy's offers the most fun for kids. Children can sit in bright jeeps and choose from a wide variety of their favorite videos to watch and older kids can play video games. The stylists are well-versed in children's haircuts and can translate any parent's cryptic description into a well-groomed or hip head. One catch: the big, enticing selection of toys (great if you're shopping by yourself for gifts). Appointments are honored in a timely manner and are recommended. Video taping is available. Cute diplomas are given to first timers.

Michael's
1263 Madison Avenue between 90th and
91st Streets
289-9612

Before Cozy's, this was the place for kiddy cuts. Real, old-time barbers are patient, friendly, and provide good cuts. Children can sit in cars or horse seats (both are old and a bit dated but the kids don't seem to mind). Big watch out: no appointments taken, which can result in waits up to one half hour on a busy Saturday. This in turn can result in temper tantrums over whose turn it is to sit in the orange car.

The Tortoise & The Hare
1470 York Avenue at 78th Street
472-3359

This spacious fun store is a good bet for a relatively calm coif. A roomy waiting area with a comfy beanbag chair and VCR is more enticing than the selection of toys. Adults will appreciate the well-placed gifts, which are virtually impossible to grab. The stylists are well equipped for diverting children with videos or games (they have a Sony Play Station, too). Appointments are recommended.

York Barber Shop
981 Lexington Avenue between 70th and
71st Streets
988-6136

For great hair without the fanfare, York Barber Shop offers a quiet, traditional setting. The barber shop pole and the line-up of authentic comfy red leather barber chairs allow parents to relive the days when kid cuts were not an amusement park. While kids may get antsy and cry in the distraction-free environment, parents will jump for joy at the price (which is significantly lower than others') and will not have to contend with tantrums over tempting toys as the shop is toy-free.

Super Cuts
410 Columbus Avenue between 79th and 80th
Streets
724-4343
1632 Second Avenue between 84th and 85th Streets
717-6363
69 University Place between 10th and 11th Streets
228-2545

It's cheap! It's crowded. It's not for grown-ups only. It's a really decent haircut.

CHAPTER 13

Who Needs a Backyard Anyway?

PLAYGROUNDS

Most suburbanites don't understand how New York City families live without backyards. However, in comparison to the city's playgrounds, a suburban backyard is boring and lonely (for moms and kids alike). Many of the city's parks offer safe equipment and fun, *relatively* clean grounds, and enough eager playmates to keep your child occupied for a few hours.

Most of us are pretty well acquainted with the playgrounds within our own neighborhoods. As creatures of habit and comfort, our tendency is to stick with the playgrounds we know; your child's playmates are there, you know where the bathroom is, and you know the tricks to round your children up to leave. However, venturing to playgrounds in the unknown can be a child-friendly way to enjoy and discover other parts of the city. So pack up the diaper bag, grab some juice boxes, snag your Metro Card, and you're on your way to swing, slide, and splash!

Down by the River

Nothing is more impressive to a three-year-old than an up-close-and-personal peek at boats cruising by. These playgrounds are the perfect place for any child to contemplate a future with the Navy.

Henry Neufeld Playground
Riverside Drive at 77th Street
Enter at 78th Street

Walk down the path to the playground. If you need to remind yourself of why you're there, just read the plaque at
the entrance: "Children, they are a miracle." This playground is a wonderful complement to a summer picnic at
the 79th Street Boat Basin. After your child has asked you
ten times for a quick dip in the Hudson, you can splash her
off with the water-spraying elephants. Also, don't forget to
bring along any older siblings. They may not be impressed
by the boat side views, but they will have fun rollerblading
or dribbling on the basketball court that's adjacent to the
playground.

Carl Schurz Playground
East End Avenue (enter on 84th Street)

At the end of Polly Gordon walk, you will find an expansive
playground, great for children of all ages (don't get nervous,
play areas are grouped by age-appropriate equipment).
Rubber ground tiles make falls relatively pain-free. Lots of
baby swings, slides, sand, and climbing apparatuses guarantee fun. During the spring and summer the park organizes
activities for small children and provides a sprinkler area.
The space is comfortable with lots of surrounding benches,
shade, and an open layout so it's easy to keep an eye on
your child without having to hover. Ice cream is available
on the way out. Also visit the esplanade behind the playground. Here, kids love to wave at boats, check out bridges,
and watch dogs. After all of this they will be fast asleep in
the stroller so you can enjoy a relaxing moment on a bench
by the river.

John Jay Park
The East River between 76th and 77th Streets

With lots of new playground equipment (it was recently renovated), this big park is a great place for children of all ages. Swings, slides, and sand for toddlers abound. Summertime is definitely fun time here. A big sprinkler area proves to be the preferred activity for most. Older children have plenty of room to rollerblade or play ball. For a larger-than-life view of tankers, walk over to 76th Street just past the basketball court. In this cul de sac, a boat passing beyond the traffic on FDR Drive is an unbelievably impressive sight.

Nelson A. Rockefeller Park
Battery Park City
Murray Street and River Terrace

The playground at Murray Street and River Terrace may be the best in the city for the under-four crowd. It's the perfect park for developing well-rounded tots. For their mega motor skills, it offers the smallest slide we have ever seen, an incredible climbing apparatus made out of mesh and wood, a cycle-go-round, and poles to slide down. For their mini motor skills, a clean sandbox and sand table. And for their budding intellects, big tic-tac-toe blocks.

Overall, this is a great year-round park. In the summer, while the children enjoy great water play with spraying elephants and rhinos, you can enjoy a cool breeze and an ocean view. In the cooler months, after the children play for a while, you can run into the Winter Garden for some hot chocolate and a break from the whipping wind.

Here's the place where you'll be reminded that Manhattan is in fact an island. The view is to die for. Unlike the views from the uptown parks, this view is quite expansive: west to New Jersey, south to The Statute of Liberty and Ellis Island, and straight down to the big boats. Your entire family can spend a sunny afternoon strolling, rollerblading, and biking down the beautiful esplanade, which runs south from Stuyvesant High School.

Hippopotamus Park
at Riverside Drive and 91st Street

With few crowds, rolling hills, and a view of the river, Riverside Park is a treat. It has lots of infant swings, seesaws, and hippos that spray water to cool kids down. The breeze off the river is cooling too, which helps to make this an easy place to spend an entire summer afternoon when it is too hot to move. The bathrooms are well maintained and safe. One watch-out: the path from the street to the park is steep, so it's slippery when wet and tough on little big-wheelers. You can also enter at 95th street, which is much less hazardous.

Musée de Swing
The idea of going to a cultural mecca can be much better than the actual visit. Inevitably, you find yourself inside the museum and before you can say, "Hey, it's Monet," your kids are ready to leave. It's swing time!

East 96th Street Playground
Fifth Avenue at East 96th Street

Located kind of near the Dana Discovery Center and the Museum of the City of New York (OK, it's not too far), this playground is tons of fun. It has lots of room for push toys, skipping and jumping, and a very clean sandbox. It also has a real tree house that's within reach of the not-too-tall climbers. And the surrounding fields are a great place to just run off some steam, but keep your eye on the kids when you do.

Ancient Playground
Fifth Avenue at East 85th Street

After a morning of art appreciation, visit this playground, located next to the Metropolitan Museum. With its sand-based surface, it offers a massive sandbox for your little digger (after a rainy day this can make for plenty of "yuck" for small children who put everything in their mouths). While tons of fun, the equipment for the active, agile two-and-up crowd can be ulcer provoking with its brick pyramids and cement tunnels.

James Michael Levin Memorial Playground
Fifth Avenue at East 76th Street

After a Frick failure and on your way to the Central Park boat pond, stop here for some big fun. Replete with a large sandbox, a fountain for water play, the ever-present bucket swings, and a roomy play area with slides and things to crawl in and hang on, it's always festively crowded here.

Spector Playground
Central Park West between 85th and 86th Streets

OK, so they weren't that interested in the dinosaurs at the Museum of Natural History. Time to find a new activity. Although this park is a few blocks further away than the Diana Ross playground at 81st Street and Central Park West, it's worth the haul. This bigger and better playground has tire swings, bridges, and slides that empty into a mega sandpit. Up on a hill, this playground is difficult to see from the street. Enter on the north side of 85th Street and walk uphill and to the left.

Park with a View
If you're in need of a visual vacation from the same old, same old neighborhood playground, it's time to venture out for a park

with a view. Whether you seek beautiful landscaping, spectacular architecture, or eclectic performers, a day at the park can only be enhanced by a new perspective on New York.

West 67th Street Playground
Central Park West between 67th and 69th Streets

Despite its name, enter the park at 69th Street to avoid the stairs. What could be more New York than horse-drawn carriages, the Tavern on the Green, and a view of the greenery of Central Park? This beautiful playground offers all of this and more. Two distinct playground areas, one for the tots and one for the four-and-up crowd, make it the perfect place for bigger families. The gate to the toddler area stays shut, so there's no need to worry about the little wanderer if you find your mind wandering in this beautiful setting.

Washington Square Park
Washington Square North between Fifth Avenue and University Place

Even though the only way you get high these days is pushing a swing into the sky, Washington Square Park can still be a great time. This newly refurbished playground has all the requisite play equipment, but what makes it extraordinary is all the activity in the park that surrounds it. A young crowd (many NYU students), jugglers, magic shows, guitar playing, even poetry readings make it a stimulating environment for all. And a peek at the World Trade Center through the arch makes for a spectacular sight.

Shop 'n Slide
Reminiscent of the days when a Saturday meant window-shopping, running errands, and a leisurely stroll to a late lunch spot, this shop 'n slide combo feels *almost* the same. These parks are strategically located near some unique shopping areas. After a romp in the park, if all goes according to plan, your children will be

snoozin' in the stroller or in such great spirits that now you can go play. . . .

Washington Market Community Park
Washington Street between Duane and
Reade Streets

A total oasis in a sea of concrete, this park looks out of place, yet feels wonderful. With green lawns and a quaint gazebo, you will forget that you are in Manhattan (if you have absolutely no peripheral vision!). The playground area is small, yet well equipped with stuff to climb, slide, and tumble. The real news here is that you can rent the gazebo for birthday parties. There are some wonderful children's shops in the area like Koh's, Just Jake's, and Shoofly as well as the nearby Winter Garden at the World Financial Center.

Bleecker Playground
At the corner of Bleecker and Hudson Streets

Who would think that a park surrounded on all four sides by whizzing traffic would be a treat for tots? The truth is that the squeals of laughter will drown out the honking horns. Brand spanking new, this delightful park has two distinct play areas: the smaller one covered in sand and the larger one with a rubberized floor. The kids may be so worn out after a romp in the park that they won't object when you want to pop into the antique stores lining Bleecker Street. If all else fails, stop into The Moon Dog Brand Ice Cream Parlor down the street.

Union Square
East 17th Street at Union Square

Fresh air and fresh fruit . . . what a pair. Your children can enjoy a romp in the well-equipped playground after you have saved massive amounts on fresh fruit, vegetables, herbs, and other organic fare. The Union Square Greenmarket is open Monday, Wednesday, Friday, and Saturday from 8 A.M. to 6 P.M. This is definitely worth the trek on a beautiful morning. Also, don't forget ABC Carpet and Home and Paragon Sports just north of the park on Broadway.

Madison Green
26th Street and Madison Avenue

One of the few benefits of waking up at the crack of dawn on weekends is having first dibs on the treasures at the Fabulous Flea Market at 26th Street and 6th Avenue. But if by 8:00 A.M. your four-year-old is ready to flee the market, check out the playground here. Enter at the Northeast corner of the park and see how quickly a tire swing and a good climb can remedy the shopping blues. Also, check out the cute doggies as they run around the walk.

Wild West Playground
Central Park West at 93rd Street

Not really F Troop, this playground has lots of fun to offer. Complete with fortresses, a sandpit, tire swings, bridges, lots of stuff to hang from, and a big sprinkler area, here, your little cowboys and Indians will be yelling *yeeehah!* by day's end. Did we mention how roomy this playground is? It's a great place for your child to test-drive her newest push-bike purchased around the corner at Albee's at Amsterdam and 95th Street.

Rudin Playground
Central Park West between 96th and 97th Streets

Even closer to Albee's is this easily accessed playground with lots to do. With tire swings, baby swings, shaded benches under big gazebos, lots of climbing apparatus for big and small children, and a sprawling sprinkler, this is a wonderful warm weather park.

CHAPTER 14

Free Play . . . But It Will Cost You

INDOOR PLAYGROUNDS

Everyone's dream on a cold or rainy day, indoor play and activity places have become New York City's answer to the suburban finished basement (but with better toys and more friends). Visits to these centers can provide a fun social setting in which your child can try new toys or activities, climb through mazes, make new friends, or just blow off some steam. Some even provide hourly baby-sitting so parents can blow off some steam, too. Most are open until 6 P.M during the week and some stay open a little later on Friday nights . . . by kiddy standards that is (oooh, 8 P.M.!). Prices range from $6 to about $9 per person. Beware: some charge for parents, too.

Playspace
2473 Broadway at 92nd Street
769-2300

Playspace is wonderful, particularly if your child is under four. The enormous playground boasts a clean sandbox, an innovative climbing jungle gym, a play kitchen (filled with appliances superior to the ones in most New York City rentals), every Little Tykes toy made, and dress-up clothes. A separate play area for small babies is stocked with age-appropriate stuff. While there is ample room, the focus at Playspace is less on running around and more on learning with new toys. The food selection is both nutritious and delicious. You are required to leave most of your belongings outside the play area, so don't bring valuables.

Kid Mazeum
80 East End Avenue at 83rd Street
327-4800

Kid Mazeum's two levels offer both physical and creative play activities. The top floor has a jungle gym complete with slides and a small separate pool of balls into which little ones can slide. The walls are brightly painted with some of your children's favorite characters such as Barney, Big Bird, and Ernie. Toddlers can ride on the mini merry-go-round (bring quarters) or just crawl around on the mats. Downstairs boasts an air castle for big jumping, stackable mats for more jumping, and a Lego room for building. For intellectual stimulation, the kids use their imaginations in the play grocery store and dress-up area (complete with video display so they can view their shows). One suggestion: don't plan on having lunch there unless you have a vending machine craving.

WonderCamp
27 West 23rd Street between Fifth and
Sixth Avenues
243-1111

WonderCamp is the perfect antidote to cramped quarters at home. The WonderNest area, designed for the four-and-under crew, has a wide variety of scaled activities including: ball pools, tunnels and slides, a Lego table with big pieces for easy handling and building, and a little merry-go-round that requires peddling by each child or one good push by an adult. WonderCamp also has scheduled activities for tots in its Club House, Craft Cabin, and Field Stage. A few things to *wonder* about: 1) Where did you spend all that money? Adults have to pay, too, and the food is a tad expensive; 2) Are the python and boa dying to slide through the play area? Their cages are awfully small. Yes, there are cages with snakes, iguanas, and turtles.

The Craft Studio
1657 Third Avenue between 92nd and 93rd Streets
831-6626

Art time can be mess time at somebody else's place—but for a price. Recommended for kids three and older, here budding artists can work with plaster, ceramic, and terracotta pottery. For a truly indulgent experience, try the chocolate molds and then you and your child can eat your creation. Don't gag, food coloring gives it that *special* hue.

Rain or Shine
115 East 29th Street between Park and
Lexington Avenues
532-4420

Whether you are an environmental activist or just looking for a place to set your young one free, this play space with a rain forest theme is sure to please. The equipment, colorful environment, and overall size of the play area is perfect for the under-four set. The upstairs has a wonderfully imaginative play area with a little stage for budding thespians and a fully stocked play house for the mommy and daddy wannabes. The ecologically correct art room boasts only recyclable materials to spark creativity. Also noteworthy is the big sandbox area complete with slide, lots of clean sand, and the calming sound of tropical birds. The downstairs has space for classes and birthday parties. The food selection is also quite good and will satisfy your little activist's snack time appetite.

Chelsea Piers
23rd Street at the Hudson River
336-6500 (Field House)

This facility encompasses what seems like every pier on the Hudson River. Depending on your child's age and abilities, she can bowl, hit golf balls, roller skate, climb a rock wall, ice skate, and shoot hoops. Just call ahead for session times, prices, and where the @#%&* to find the activity.

CHAPTER 15

Kiddy Kulture

CULTURAL ACTIVITIES

New York is the cultural capital of the world. It was true when you were single and it's just as true now that you are a family. Except, these days, with kids in tow, culture comes in unexpected packages.

It's no longer about looking at Byzantine art in the Pierpont Morgan Museum but rather about pitching pennies into the wishing pools at the Met. It's no longer about four hour operas in Italian but about lollipop concerts at noon. It's no longer about sunbathing in Sheep Meadow but about teaching your child to ride a bike on Literary Walk.

A Walk in the Park

Central Park. A crown jewel. A backyard. An entertainment center. A place to chat with the animals, toss a ball, sit on the grass, twirl on a carousel, play checkers, fly a kite, see a concert, catch fireflies, blow off steam, climb rocks, play with friends, learn to ride a bike, study nature, be noisy, be silly, be quiet, or just sleep in a stroller.

A walk in Central Park can be both a cultural outing and an opportunity for good old-fashioned, relaxing fun. We've guided you to the landmarks, but plenty more is waiting to be discovered. So, put on your walking shoes, get adventurous, and explore, explore, explore.

The Carousel
Mid-Park between 64th and 65th Streets
879-0244

What can we say? Nothing is more touching than watching your little one enjoy one of New York City's greatest treasures. Built in 1908, this carousel is one of the largest in the United States. Help your tot hop on one of the fifty-eight hand-carved horses and go for the brass ring. Make sure you have plenty of film in your camera. Balloons, popcorn, cotton candy, and tons of other children make this a virtual carnival for kids. The carousel is open seven days a week, weather permitting.

The Dairy
Mid-Park at 65th Street
(West of the Carousel)

Across from the carousel, this gingerbread type house has a great Central Park map out front. The Dairy offers slide-shows, exhibits, and programs on park history and design. If you're planning an entire day in the park, this is a great place to start. There's also a gift shop.

The Chess & Checkers House
Mid-Park at 65th Street
(West of the Carousel)

Diagonal to the Dairy, this open-air shelter sits atop a large rock outcrop and boasts tons of chess and checkers tables. You can borrow playing pieces from the Dairy's information desk. You would think chess and checkers would be sedentary activities, but your climb up to the top may well be your exercise for the day.

Central Park Wildlife Center (The Zoo)
East Side of the Park between 59th and
64th Streets
861-6030

Look up! The amazing Delacorte clock welcomes your child to the zoo with its spectacular animated figures that chime on the hour and half-hour. In the newly renovated, wilderness-simulated environments, the animals look content. We did hear, however, that one of the polar bears needed some peanut butter therapy. (Don't we all?)

This zoo will make your child feel as though he's playing with the animals. He can race the sea lions as they swim laps in their circular glass tank. He can go nose to nose with the polar bears as they eat, swim, and play in their frosty habitat (of course, glass separates him from the bears). He'll be so close to the monkeys, he'll feel as though the mommy orangutan is picking nits off of him when it's really just you wiping ice cream out of his hair.

The Tisch Children's Zoo at the Central Park Wildlife Center
Enter Central Park at 64th Street

Catering to New York families with small children, this brand new children's (mostly petting) zoo across the way will be on your list of places to go again and again. Putting your child's delight aside for a moment, New York parents will truly appreciate the zoo's setup and subtle amenities. First of all, there's a stroller check right outside the gate (under the tunnel) that's free and safe. Secondly, the zoo area is so small that you can actually have a nice "uppy-free" stroll with your tot. And lastly, the bathrooms are right there—no spastic sprints in search of the potty. Now, as for the zoo itself, it's fabulous. Aside from the requisite farm animals to pet and feed, children can leap on the lily pads like a frog, get tangled in a spider web like a frantic fly, and try on a tortoise shell for size. The exhibits are really inventive and sized perfectly for independent discoveries.

The Boat Pond
East Side of Park at 74th Street

A serene yet bustling oasis in Central Park, this place lets you feel like you've left the city. Children are delighted by the parade of exact replica sailboats that sail on the pond. In good weather, you can rent a model sailboat, which your child sails by remote control. Stroll over to the Alice in Wonderland statue where children love to climb over and under Alice and her friends (especially the mushrooms). The snack shack offers everything from hot dogs to hot chocolate, depending on the season.

Literary Walk
Mid-Park between 66th and 72nd Streets
(Walk South from Bethesda Fountain)

There's no better place than here to teach your child how to ride her bike. Beneath the canopy of elm trees and alongside statues of literary greats you'll find a quintessential New York experience. And if you feel like you're in a movie, it's probably because you saw this scene in *Kramer vs. Kramer*.

Bethesda Fountain
Mid-Park at 72nd Street

A beautiful fountain set below the road, its backdrop is a tranquil pond and lush forest. The Bethesda angel perched atop the fountain is symbolic of the beauty and tranquility of Central Park. You can watch dogs bathe in the fountain, sometimes hear great music, and, of course, on weekend afternoons be entertained by the Crows at the top of the stairs.

The Crows
72nd Street Cut-through above the Bethesda Fountain

A lively, athletic group of men manipulate oversized crow puppets of all shapes and sizes to foot-tappin' tunes. They draw quite a crowd on weekend afternoons, especially passersby with tiny tots. Don't forget to drop some change in their tip bucket—these guys are really nice and work hard in the hot sun.

The Lake
West Side of Park between 71st and 77th Streets

Make way for ducklings! Here your little one can feed not only cute duckies but also foul fowl like pigeons. They can climb on the rocks and picnic by the pond, making for a pleasant afternoon respite.

Belvedere Castle
Mid-Park at 79th Street

After huffing and puffing your way up many stairs with tots in tow, you are rewarded with an extraordinary 360-degree panoramic view of Central Park and New York City from the top of the castle. The magnificent Midtown skyline contrasts with the tranquil Turtle Pond. The castle also houses the Henry Luce Nature Observancy, which offers nature activities in the park. Call 772-0210 for more information.

Dana Discovery Center
East Side of Park at 110th Street
near Harlem Meer
860-1370

Located at the very tippety-top of Central Park, this gingerbread house seems as though it's floating in the surrounding
pond. As its name and location implies, it is a center devoted to helping children discover nature, by hosting exhi-
bitions in its downstairs gallery and creative workshops in
a large room upstairs. Believing that all of Central Park is
a wonder waiting to be discovered, the center also sponsors
nature walks in and around Harlem Meer. Don't miss two
brand-new playgrounds: one right outside the center's door
and the other two blocks south at 108th Street and Fifth
Avenue.

Pee Pee or Picasso

Museums—not just children's museums—can provide a wonderful experience for both parent and child. You'll be surprised by
how much a one-year-old can enjoy an art museum. While they
won't pontificate on impressionism and neoclassicism, they'll find
wonder in the colors, shapes, and texture of the art and the echoes
of the wide-open halls.

Children's Museum of Manhattan
212 West 83rd Street between Amsterdam
and Broadway
721-1223

This highly interactive child-friendly environment offers
hours of fun and play for the one-and-up set. In addition to
wonderful exhibits (recent ones have included the world's
largest Pooh or the wonderful world of Dr. Seuss), the museum includes a toddler playroom that offers children a preschool like environment in which to play with puzzles, look
at the fish tank, take a spin down the slide, and find new

playmates. Check for workshops and classes. The watch-outs are 1) weekends have waits up to a half hour, and 2) the lobby gift shop is an expensive kid magnet.

The Metropolitan Museum of Art
Fifth Avenue at 82nd Street
535-7710

Having children does not mean you have to give up all those Saturdays of adult culture. Children are in awe of the enormous thirty-two–acre space, which contrasts sharply with a 1,000 square foot apartment. The Egyptian wing with the Temple of Dendur and wishing pools (bring pennies), the Sculpture Garden, and the Arms and Armor Hall are equally fascinating for you and your tot. The museum makes it easy to bring your children. To the left of the main entrance, just drop off your stroller, pick up a baby backpack, and you're set. Also, keep in mind that the Met offers a twelve-session parent/child workshop for children ages three to five years. The classes allow you both to engage in the process of creating while learning about the museum's works of art.

Children's Museum of the Arts
72 Spring Street between Crosby and
Lafayette Street
274-0986

If you have your heart set on an afternoon in SoHo or live in the area, this museum can be a great kiddy pit stop. This incredibly interactive museum is more like an artistic playground. The museum boasts a variety of areas in which children can jump into the Monet Ball Pool, create pictures in the Chalk It Up wall-to-wall chalkboard area, or manipulate the colorful, interesting magnets in the Magnetic Masterpieces room. The environment is inspiring from top to bottom; it's full of colorful creations such as children's art, papier-mâché animals, and imaginatively bejeweled chandeliers. At the time of this writing, the museum was moving, so call for the new address.

Guggenheim Museum
1071 Fifth Avenue between 88th and
89th Streets
423-3500

While your child is testing out this Frank Lloyd Wright masterpiece as an Olympic-sized ramp, you can be experiencing some of the finest art in the world. Brightly colored paintings and life-sized sculptures can be viewed up close and from all angles, providing a wonderful introduction to art for your child.

The American Museum of Natural History
Central Park West and 79th Street
769-5100

In the days when the dinosaurs roamed free . . . it had to feel something like this museum. The sheer size of the animals displayed here is enough to wow even the most cynical New York child. A staple on the "Mommy I'm bored!" suggestion list, most New York parents cannot keep track of how many times they've been here. And for the average three-year-old who doesn't yet understand the concept of taxidermy, this may be a better option than the Bronx Zoo. The lines at the Central Park West (CPW) entrance can be frightening on the weekends, so try entering the museum on the ground level at 77th Street between CPW and Columbus. Also, strollers are welcomed.

Intrepid Sea Air Space Museum
West Side Highway at West 46th Street
Pier 86
245-2533

The Intrepid Museum can be so much more than just a spot where your child oohs and ahhs as you zoom down the West Side Highway. Just park at Pier 86, head up to the deck for a long look, and climb on up the myriad of fascinating planes and hear your child say "Zoooom."

The New York City Fire Museum
278 Spring Street between Hudson and
Varick Street
691-1303

This place takes the trauma out of your child's obsession with fire trucks. No blaring sirens. No screeching trucks. No wondering where the fire is. Just plenty of fascination and satisfaction. A 1901 horse-drawn engine and an 1857 hand-pulled hose carriage are two of many pieces of antique fire equipment to be enjoyed here. The gift shop has everything from hats, T-shirts, and patches to mini trucks, videos, and books. Recommended for the three-and-up crowd (your two-year-old may be too frustrated that he can't climb aboard).

New York City Local Fire Houses

The perfect environment to satisfy even the most fire engine–obsessed right in your own neighborhood. More often than not, the fire fighters of your local firehouse have an open door policy when it comes to kids. When not putting out fires, they frequently let the kids ogle the equipment and even climb aboard. And by the way, they are among the city's finest . . . looking, that is.

Museum of the City of New York
1220 Fifth Avenue at 103rd Street
534-1672

If your budding art history professor isn't quite ready for a
day at the Guggenheim but has been to the Children's Museum more times than she can remember, stop here for a
quick visit. This is definitely not a hands-on museum, but it
can teach kids that just looking at neat things can be fun
too. The doll house exhibit on the second floor is a charming trip through time and the marine gallery can be fun for
the four-and-up set.

National Museum of the American Indian
George Gustav Heye Center
1 Bowling Green
668-6624

A great opportunity to teach your children about an important part of their American heritage in an incredibly
beautiful setting. The displays feature moccasins, masks,
and headdresses; they're colorful, sometimes scary, and
will certainly make your child forget that this is a history
lesson too. The gift shop is an adventure on its own with
rawhide rattles, pop-up books, and rubber buffalo. Enter
the museum at the gift shop level to avoid a staircase that
can make even the fittest hyperventilate.

Showtime
Since most children are used to being center stage at home, a
trip to a children's theater can be a humbling experience. However,
there's no need to risk a $50 ticket to Broadway when many rea-
sonably priced, entertaining children's shows are available on other
less famous streets in the city. These eclectic productions, many of
which change weekly, include things like magic, music, storytelling,
clowns, and puppet shows. Many of the shows encourage audience
participation, which can be a treat for your aspiring "Annie."
Some of these listings feature children's programs only. Others

have both adult and children's productions. All of them, however, have schedules that vary frequently. Check with each for current shows, show times, and ticket prices.

Big Apple Circus
Lincoln Center Plaza
268-2500
October through January

A circus with class? This isn't an oxymoron when you're talking about The Big Apple Circus. Clowns, elephants, horses, and dogs at close range make it a treat for any two-year-old. But when you add in wonderful acrobatics, "How'd they do that?" magic, and some real humor, even parents will eagerly look forward to next year's show.

Grove Street Playhouse
39 Grove Street
741-6346

Originally the Little People's Theater Company, Miss Magesties is the oldest children's theater company in New York. The shows, however, are innovative, wacky, and wonderful for children ages two to twelve. Fun adaptations of classic fairy tales in an interactive and intimate environment (only seventy-four seats) make this a memorable experience.

The Knitting Factory
74 Leonard Street between Broadway and
Church Streets
877-6115

With only a few traces from the evening before, this downtown bar and band haven transforms itself into a wonderful children's theater each Saturday afternoon. The eclectic productions, which change weekly, run the gamut from magic to music to storytelling to clowns to puppet shows. Many of the shows require audience participation and offer opportunities for the not-so-shy to experience life on the stage. Also visit the sister theater, West End Children's Theater, at 2911 Broadway (between 113th and 114th streets).

Lenny Suib Puppet Playhouse
Asphalt Green/Murphy Center
555 East 90th Street off of York Avenue
369-8890

Only when you have children would you consider going to the theater at 10:30 A.M. This intimate theater is the perfect entree into the performing arts for two-and three-year-olds. Weekly shows run the gamut from puppets and marionettes to magicians and storytelling.

Little Orchestra Society
Lollipop Concerts
Francis Gould Hall at the French Institute
55 East 59th Street at Lincoln Center
704-2100

What a wonderful introduction to music appreciation. It's the ABC's of classical music with an animal twist. What child could possibly yearn for Barney when the wind instrument is represented by Toot the Bird? A series of three for any three-year-old is sure to please.

The Puppet Company
The Al E. Gator Show
31 Union Square West at 16th Street
Loft 2B
741-1646

With inventive puppets, a small intimate space, and in-theater munching allowed, this show is a perfect weekend pit stop (it's roughly forty-five minutes long). The atmosphere is wonderfully casual—it's almost like dropping by the house of a friend who happens to be a puppeteer (they even patiently waited for latecomers). The show itself has something for everyone—humor that adults will appreciate, and puppets that will wow the children. The space and the show are both available for birthdays.

Rug Concerts
Diller-Quaile School of Music
24 East 95th Street between Madison & 5th Avenues
369-1484

It literally is a concert on a rug, and a great opportunity to have your child learn about music in an intimate, relaxed, and kid-friendly environment. At each of the concerts, children will learn about instruments from diverse periods and cultures. Since everyone is on the same rug, your child will feel close to the music. There are several concerts throughout the school year.

Swedish Cottage Marionette Theater
Central Park West and 81st Street

Puppets on strings so close to the swings! Located in a charming, rustic theater in Central Park, it's the furthest from the theater district you can get and still be entertained splendidly. Children are exposed to a variety of puppets as the show combines marionette, hand, and shadow puppets.

Parents will have to temporarily cut their strings, as the children sit up close and you, being so big, can't sit with them. Shows are twice daily at 10:30 A.M. and noon and reservations are required. With only one show a year, you may think you can only go once. But then think about how many times a week your three-year-old can sit through Muppet Classic Theater.

Sylvia and Danny Kaye Playhouse
695 Park Avenue at 68th Street
772-4448

The Sylvia and Danny Kaye Playhouse hosts the infamous Paper Bag Players during the winter months (usually December through March). For the environmentally conscious tot, children can learn about recycling in a fun and lively form. With 624 seats, the show is not intimate, but it is interactive. It's incredible to think that hundreds of children can be inspired to sing and dance for paper bags and corrugated cardboard.

TADA!
120 West 28th Street between 6th & 7th Avenues
627-1732

If your three-year-old thinks great children's theater is a massive temper tantrum, a trip to TADA! will quickly cure this misconception. A theater for children and of children, TADA's shows are actually performed by children ages seven to seventeen. Each year, TADA! features three main shows (mostly musicals), one smaller-scale production, and five staged readings. While the musicals are appropriate for three-to five year-olds, the other performances are recommended for children over six. Unlike many other children's theaters, they are open during the week in the summer months.

13th Street Repertory Company
50 West 13th Street between 5th and 6th Avenues
675-6677

Twenty-five years ago Edith O'Hara founded this company
based on the belief that if children get involved in theater
at a young age, they will have a life-long appreciation for it.
The sixty-five seat theater is conducive to audience participation. Children can get so involved that they wind up on
stage in many of the productions. From fairy tales to farm
stories, your child will have plenty of opportunity to test
her star potential. In fact, two of Edith's daughters have
performed on Broadway.

Summer in the City

SUMMER ACTIVITIES

Even if you do not spend the rest of the year trying to rationalize child rearing in New York City, steamy summers can bring out the paternal guilt in just about everyone. However, rid yourself of all pessimistic thoughts immediately and bear in mind the following:

➡ The population just about halves itself.

➡ The parks couldn't be better (many with water sprinklers).

➡ Ice cream trucks are parked just about everywhere.

➡ Street fairs are in full force.

➡ Rarely do you experience the burning sensation of the inside of a car that has been roasting in the sun for hours.

For daily activity, several camps offer your preschooler a fun-filled summer. Also, most program centers offer summer sessions of their regularly scheduled classes.

Last, but not least, wonderful outdoor concerts and activities occur throughout the city. Where else can you end a hectic day with a family picnic in Central Park while listening to the New York Philharmonic?

It's So Campy

You won't believe how many really good camps for toddlers exist in New York. Nevertheless, finding one can be frustrating, as most of the well-known camps don't start taking children until the summer before they enter kindergarten (children turning age five).

While it may not be the same as your experience at Camp Sokittoome, these camps will accept your two-and-a-half-year-old and will provide lots of campy things to do. The camp day, for camps listed, is at least two hours long and parents aren't invited. For an almost-three-year-old who will be off to preschool in the fall, these camps can provide a great transition to that experience. Check with each camp for fee schedules and session dates.

Also check out local preschools, not just the one your child will be attending. Several offer excellent summer fun in well funded facilities, and they are open to all. If your child isn't quite ready for camp, remember your local program centers.

CATS Summer Program
Central Presbyterian
593 Park Avenue between 63rd and 64th Streets
751-4876
Ages: three to four years

Running around all summer without breaking a sweat, CATS offers every sport under the sun—inside with lots of air conditioning. Arts & crafts and storytelling round out the three-hour program. Camp hours are 9 A.M. to noon, Monday through Friday. Just wait until they turn five to graduate to the CATS Summer Tennis & Sports Day Camp located at Columbia University.

Church Street School for Music & Art
74 Warren Street
571-7290
Ages: three-and-a-half to five years

The focus here is musical and artsy. Their music program uses the Dalcroze method, which teaches music through movement. Teachers use parachutes, scarves, and hoops as aids in teaching scales and other music theory concepts. Their art program emphasizes process, not product. Teachers use various tools such as clay, paint, sculpture, collage, paint brushes, and fingers to create. Camp hours are 9:30 A.M. to 12:30 P.M. Campers attend one to four days per week, Monday through Thursday.

Columbus Gym
606 Columbus Avenue between 89th and
90th Streets
721-0900
Ages: two-and-a-half to five

After spending an activity-filled day at Columbus Gym, your child is sure to sleep well at night. With its top notch gymnastics program (including an Olympic-sized trampoline), terrific outside roofdeck (with lots of water play for cooling off), and animated friendly staff, Columbus Gym is a wonderful option for children starting at age two-and-a-half. Mini campers can attend the program from four to ten weeks. The youngest campers attend three days from 9 A.M. to 12 P.M. and the three to fives go full force—five days until 1 P.M. or 3 P.M.

Discovery Programs West
251 West 100th Street at West End Avenue
749-8717
Ages: two-and-a-half to five years

Like its year-round programs, the summer program here is low key and fun for toddlers. In the On My Own Program, your two-and-a-half-year-old doesn't have to wait for July 4th for a little independence. This two-hour separation program is offered from one to five days per week. At the Mini Camp, three- to five-year-olds can experience it all under and on top of one roof. Indoor activities include cooking, art & crafts, and gymnastics. Children can enjoy some summer sun splashing, spraying, playing, and picnicking on the large roof. For sleepy heads, the Mini Camp's 10:30 A.M. start time is an added bonus.

The 53rd Street YWCA
610 Lexington Avenue at 53rd Street
735-9702
Ages: four to five years for SummerTOTS Program

This camp offers organized activities including music, pre-gymnastics, arts & crafts, dance/movement, swimming, and theater games. Field trips are on Fridays. At the end of each month, the campers invite parents to a lunchtime performance. The camp does not provide transportation. Camp hours are 9:00 A.M. to 5:30 P.M. They also offer extended hours as follows: early drop-off from 8:30 A.M. and late pickup until 6:00 P.M. This program is limited to sixteen children.

Greenwich House Music School
46 Barrow Street
242-4770
Ages: three and four years only

A tranquil block and a quaint brownstone are the perfect setting for this summer camp. In the school's backyard, children have free play and swim time (wading pool). They also enjoy music and art classes, snacks and storytelling. Children attend for three hours per day, 9:30 A.M. to 12:30 P.M., five days per week.

92nd Street Y
1395 Lexington Avenue between 91st and
92nd Streets
427-9831
Ages: three to five years for the K 'Ton Ton
program

The Y is a full-service summer camp that offers your children arts & crafts, music, movement, dramatic play, and swimming. Parents arrange for transportation directly with a bus company recommended by the 92nd Street Y. Camp hours are 9 A.M. to 12 P.M. for three-year-olds and 9 A.M. to 3 P.M. for five-year-olds. All activities take place at the 92nd Street Y facilities, both inside and outside. There are no field trips.

Rodeph Shalom Summer Camp
7 West 83rd Street between Central Park West
and Columbus Avenue
362-8800
Ages: two years nine months to five years

Camp at Rodeph Shalom offers tons of summer fun for your children. With Rodeph's spacious and high quality facilities at their disposal, campers can cook, sing, dance, and enjoy story time both in and out of doors. Here, no week is exactly the same. Children can enjoy different themes such as puppet week, circus week, and farm week. The camp day is from 9 A.M. to 1 P.M. and campers can attend for just one week or for the entire seven-week session.

74th Street Magic Summer Days Camp
510 East 74th Street
737-3070
Ages: three to six years

74th Street Magic offers your children a program including arts & crafts, music, creative movement, story time, cooking, nature study, group games, outdoor games, wading pools, and sprinklers. This camp does not have a pool and no transportation is provided. Camp hours are either 9 A.M. to 12 P.M. or 9 A.M. to 3 P.M. daily.

Sol Goldman Y
New Town Day Camp
344 East 14th Street
780-0800
Ages: two years nine months to six years

This camp's program offerings include music, drama, arts & crafts, story time, block building, rooftop playground, sprinklers, and weekly field trips. Camp meets Monday through Friday and their hours are 8:30 A.M. to 4 P.M. or 8:30 A.M. to 1 P.M. (half-day). Oneg Shabbat is celebrated every week. The camp provides snacks, trips, cookouts, and a camp T-shirt.

Summer Breeze
1520 York Avenue at 80th Street
734-0922
Ages: two- to three-and-a-half years

This place may seem familiar. That's because this camp makes use of the wonderful facilities found at Gymtime Gymnastics, Rhythm & Glues, and York Avenue Preschool. So, instead of a forty-five minute session of gym or art, you get a fun-filled day with activities like music, cooking, drama, games, storytelling, splashing, and outdoor play.

SummerSault
The Town School
540 East 76th Street
288-0740
Ages: two years eight months to nine years

This camp offers swimming, tumbling, music, arts & crafts, and a rooftop playground. Everyone participates in Whimsical Wednesdays, which have included Teddy Bear Day, Fiesta Day, musical performances, Hat/Pajama Day, and a carnival. Camp hours are full-day: 9 A.M. to 3 P.M., Monday through Thursday, 9 A.M. to 12 P.M. on Friday. Half-days are 9 A.M. to 12 P.M. The camp provides trips, cookouts, and a camp T-shirt. There are sixteen to eighteen children per group in the Bronze Division (three- and four-year-olds).

Out in the Open

Concerts in the Park
The Great Lawn
Enter Central Park at 85th Street
Behind The Metropolitan Museum

There is nothing like listening to the New York Philharmonic outdoors with the Belvedere Castle and the silhouette of the Upper West Side and beyond as the backdrop. And best of all, your children are free to roam, spill, and play. However, the only wine that is welcome here comes in a bottle—most high-pitched whines clash with Beethoven's Fifth. Two big tips: the early bird gets the best blanket space and if you are meeting people, choose an original marker so they can find you—no balloons in primary colors.

SummerStage
Enter Central Park at East 72nd Street
360-2777

Some enchanted evening! It's beautiful. It's breezy. Your child is catching fireflies. You're listening to some of the most incredible music in the world. If you come often enough, your child is going to be exposed to everything from reggae to opera while you are gazing up at the Manhattan skyline. Come early with a blanket and a picnic basket and be prepared to have a good time.

The Museum of Modern Art
11 West 53rd Street between Fifth and
Sixth Avenues
708-9807

This museum boasts a beautifully spacious backyard garden where they host concerts in the summer. Bring the whole family and enjoy classical concerts under the stars. It's best to bring along snacks for your young ones—unless they dig Brie and Perrier.

The Cooper-Hewitt Museum
2 East 91st Street at Fifth Avenue
860-6868

One of the last great mansions on Fifth Avenue plays host to a July outdoor concert series. The program is wonderfully varied—it can range from a Haitian Drum troupe to jazz, classical, or rock guitar. Each concert is preceded by a lecture. Isn't it nice to have an excuse to skip it? They love to see young faces here, but don't plan on breaking in your new picnic basket. Stop into Pintaile's Pizza before you come here.

Bryant Park
42nd Street between Fifth and Sixth Avenues
Bryant Park Restoration Corporation
983-4142

Plan a lunchtime or after 5 P.M. break from work and meet your child here for music, movies, and more. Newly renovated and quite beautiful, Bryant Park is a flowering oasis in the heart of midtown west. Catch the Words & Music festival where young people from all over the city sing, dance, and play musical instruments. Well-known musicians play classical music at lunchtime. Classic films are shown every Monday at dusk. Call for more information and a schedule of activities.

Pershing Square Park
Park Avenue between 41st and 42nd Streets
Bryant Park Restoration Corporation
983-4142

Musical performances galore take place mostly at lunchtime. You can celebrate Cinco de Mayo or listen to the Double Dutch Divas with your little one in nice weather, and when you need a break from the work grind and your child needs a parent fix. And you'll go back to the office with a smile on your face and smelling like coconut oil. Call for more information and a schedule of activities.

The MetLife Building
200 Park Avenue
Bryant Park Restoration Corporation
983-4142

Another site for the Words & Music festival, here you can find lunchtime performances by various school choirs and the Joffrey Concert Dancers, among others. Have your babysitter or your spouse bring your tot—you bring lunch. Don't forget that Mister Softy idles at the curb. Call for more information and a schedule of activities.

Grucci Fireworks at the Macy's Fourth of July
Celebration
Go to the FDR Drive in the midtown area
and look up

Bang! This is the only time you don't hit the dirt when you
hear this noise. These world-renowned fireworks are magnificent. Don't forget to buy a hot dog and a twirly pinwheel
for your tot. And stay upwind from the display so you're
not eating ash with your hot dog.

CHAPTER 17

Sirens Ringin'
Can You Hear Them?

WINTER ACTIVITIES

Whether you escape to a park with your Radio Flyer, strap on your skates beneath gilded statues, or find a hidden hot spot, this city is hoppin' with fun things to do in the winter. Not everything requires a good snowfall or spending lots of money. Sometimes all that is required is a good attitude.

Sledding Locations—You'd Be Surprised!

West Street & Vesey Street

Perched on a gently rolling hill by the World Financial Center, young kids get a thrill sledding. Bundle up, because the wind off the water can sometimes be fierce.

FDR Drive, near Exit 3 (South Street)

We spotted a gaggle of children sledding here after a four-inch snowstorm. The kids were having a ball and the scenery is picturesque.

Central Park, various locations

Just enter the park and listen for peals of laughter and de-lighted screams. Head in that direction. New Yorkers are an enterprising lot and when it snows, virtually every hill becomes a magnet for the Radio Flyer/neon plastic saucer set. Dog Hill and Cedar Hill are known as great sledding spots (near 79th/80th Streets on the East Side).

Riverside Drive Park

West Siders are friendly and neighborly, and it really shows when everyone is in Riverside Park. The best locations in-clude the hills between 79th and 84th Streets and, for the true speed seekers, check out the hills near the Hippo play-ground (91st Street).

Skating—Trust Us, Your Skates from Grade School Don't Cut It!

Rockefeller Center
601 Fifth Avenue
332-7654

Beneath gilded statues and a massive Christmas tree, this is a beautiful spot to twirl around on the ice. Don't bother going on the weekends. Rather, arrive on a Tuesday in the early evening to avoid the lines. Bundle up—the wind whips here. Skate rental available.

Wollman Rink
Central Park, north of 59th Street at 6th Avenue
396-1010

More workhorse than work of art, this is a huge outdoor rink replete with lockers, fast food, and lots of people. Be prepared to skate to an eclectic mix of music and to shield younger tots from careening teenagers. Skate rental available.

The Ice Studio
1034 Lexington Avenue between 73rd and 74th
Streets
535-0304

A tiny indoor rink perfect for first ice skating experiences. Your tiny tot will love venturing out onto the ice with her first pair of shiny skates. The Ice Studio offers group kiddy instruction for three- to-five-year-olds and general skating at various times throughout the week. They don't offer any food here and discourage you from bringing your own. But, don't worry, the average skate only lasts an hour. Call for information on skate times and fees. Skate rental available (smallest is children's size 8).

Sky Rink at Chelsea Piers
Pier 62, 23rd Street at Hudson River
336-6100

Brand-spanking new, these two enormous rinks will make you forget that you are in congested New York. They have extensive skating lessons, an above-average snack center, and relatively new skates to rent. (What a treat!) Don't bother walking there; either take a cab or the bus.

Celebrations—Libations Will Have to Wait!

Tree Lighting at Rockefeller Center
Fifth Avenue at 50th Street

A New York institution, this ceremony takes place in and around the rink at Rockefeller Center in the beginning of December. Hoards of people attend, but everyone is in an incredibly festive mood. Except, of course, for those commuters trying to fight the crowds to make a 6:15 P.M. train at Grand Central. Just avoid them. Bundle up—a cold wind blows from the river.

Menorah Lighting in front of the Plaza Hotel
Fifth Avenue at 59th Street

You can't miss the enormous menorah out in front of the Plaza Hotel. A lovely ceremony marks the first night of candle lighting, and a new candle is lit each evening until the end of Hanukkah. The hotel is conveniently located across the street from F. A. O. Schwarz, where you can stop in for last-minute gift-buying or for some delectable confections; jars and jars of your old favorites line the walls in their candy store on the second floor. Not surprisingly, F. A. O. Schwarz stays open late during the holidays. For more information about the menorah lighting, call the Parks Department, Special Events at 408-0226.

CHAPTER 18

Over the River and
Through the Tunnel

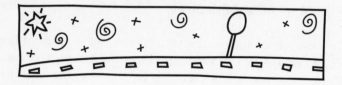

QUICK TRIPS

Enough about what's what in Manhattan. Here are some fun and easy things to do if you need to get out. Do not worry, no need to spend hours on a train or in the car, since there is plenty to do less than an hour away.

Sometimes these little trips can be both fun and fun . . . ctional. So, if you have some major shopping to do with kids in tow, consider a road trip, which can be more convenient and economical. Call ahead for directions.

Fun Trips

The Bronx Zoo
Bronx River Parkway at Fordham Road
718-367-1010

While only twenty minutes away, it feels like miles. In its 265-acre wooded setting, children and animals alike roam free. The children's zoo area offers an up close and personal experience for the under fours (even six-year-olds think it's lots of fun).

Here, it's OK for your kids to act like animals. In fact, it's encouraged. They can climb on the monkey bars, pop their heads out of the gopher hole, and get tangled in the spider web. If you have an older child with you, regress and use/borrow a double stroller . . . it's a lot of walking! When it's time to feed your little animals, you'll be happier if you packed your own—the food is junky and expensive.

Wave Hill
Independence Avenue at 249th Street
Riverdale, the Bronx
718-549-3200

Twenty minutes from the madness of midtown is pure serenity at Wave Hill. Gardens, flowers, rolling lawns, and a view to boot provide a wonderful place for a family picnic. However, don't bring any of the usual playtime paraphernalia. Balls and bikes are no-nos, but giggles and wide-open space can be enough. At the Kerlin Learning Center (located in the basement of the main building), children can enjoy the colors of nature and the freedom of space while doing a family art project. Rain or shine, they offer a host of weekend activities led by an enthusiastic and engaging staff.

Liberty Science Center
Liberty State Park
251 Philip Street, Jersey City
201-200-1000

Just a ten-minute car trip outside the Holland Tunnel will prove to you that the biggest cockroach is not in New York City. Home of the Costa Rican Cucaracha, this center is full of wonderful interactive exhibits that will engage the two-and-up child for hours. Highlights include the Invention Space full of Legos, building blocks, and gyroscopes, and the touch tank where you and your child can handle a spider crab, giant insects, or baby snakes (eek!).

Queens County Farm Museum
73-50 Little Neck Parkway, Floral Park
718-347-FARM

A forty-seven–acre farm in Queens? It's a surprise to most that this farm exists so close to the city—just about thirty minutes by car. Don't be fooled by the "museum" designation. In addition to the landmark farmhouse, your children can see enough animals to rival any rendition of "Old MacDonald's Farm." Oh, and the visit is free (hayrides are a nominal amount). Ask for a yearly calendar of events, which include activities such as a Barnyard Easter Egg Hunt, Apple Festival, and Children's Fall Festival.

New York Botanical Gardens
200th Street and Southern Boulevard
718-817-8616

Who needs a windowbox in Chappaqua when you have this in the Bronx? Aside from child specific activities, just a stroll around the magnificent grounds is sure to delight. For instance, the Big Bugs, which include a twenty-five foot grasshopper sculpture, is far more fascinating than your average two-inch cockroach. And at the Family Garden (soon to be part of the new eight-acre Everett Children's Adventure Garden) no thumb is too small to be green. Children can experience it all . . . including planting and harvesting with pint-sized garden tools. Programs vary according to the season with both indoor and outdoor activities. And no matter how kind, most parents won't be able to resist chanting "redrum, redrum" while their child is trapped in Beth's Maze.

Aquarium for Wildlife Conservation
West 8th Street and Surf Avenue
Coney Island, Brooklyn
718-265-3400

"Yeah! We're going to see the Fishies!" While most tots will be expecting a big carton of Pepperidge Farm cheddar snacks, they will be overjoyed at the sight of the real thing. With a big tank of Beluga whales, dolphins, sea lions (quite a tired bunch), and lots of little tanks to press up to for a close look, your child may never feel the same about downing a handful of cheddar fishies. For lunch, just drive around the corner to Nathan's for famous hot dogs and unbelievable fries.

Silverman's Farm
451 Sport Hill Road
Easton, Connecticut
203-261-3306

If Halloween's around the corner, it's time to head north to Silverman's Farm. While few city kids have a front stoop to show off their carvings, they still deserve to pick from the cream of the crop. Silverman's Farm will give them plenty of pumpkins to choose from—enough to fill your entire apartment. The hayrides are among the best and bumpiest and are sure to remind hay fever sufferers why they love living in the city. Other attractions include a big animal farm (beware of the bees), a picnic area (bring your own), and a market with lots of fresh farm goodies. When you check out, guess your pumpkin's weight and it's free! (Just make sure you weigh your tot before you go for reference.) Columbus Day tends to be very crowded; avoid it.

The Maritime Aquarium
10 North Water Street
South Norwalk, Connecticut 06854
203-852-0700

With lots of room to run around and plenty to see and touch, this destination is fun year round. The center has activities and exhibits that are wonderfully age-appropriate for the under-four crew. Favorites include the indoor seal feedings and nature discussions in an intimate setting, the Jellyfish Room, the Tent exhibits (e.g., robotic bats), and a shark tank. Children can learn a lot of fishy stuff here. Who can think of a more exciting way to learn to count than lying on top of the flounder tank chanting "One fishy, two fish-ies. . . ." Stop and chat with the senior volunteers who know anything and everything about the fish. Lunch here can be a treat as tots are unlikely to make the connection between the sea life and the chowder you are slurping.

New York Hall of Science
47-01 111th Street at 46th Avenue
Flushing Meadows
718-699-0005

If it's your three-year-old's turn to tag along with big sis, she'll find plenty to do here. While primarily geared to the post-kindergarten set, there are special areas that are just right for preschoolers, such as the Make It and Take It area and The Preschool Discovery Place. Both offer intimate environments in which children can do art projects, participate in some constructive play, or go eye-to-eye with some serious creepy crawlers. If none of the aforementioned seems worth the trip, the bubble table is a definite draw. Your child will be amazed that he can make bubbles as big as he is. And if you find yourself stumped by the nineteenth *why*, just deposit your child next to the nearest explainer.

Fun . . . ctional Trips

Toys 'R Us
Plaza 48 Shopping Center (48th Street off of
Northern Blvd.), Long Island City
718-937-8697

For holiday shopping, it can be a lot easier to load up the trunk in the parking lot than to shlep around the city. Savings are significant relative to most Manhattan toy stores. And though Toys 'R Us stores can be found in town, cab rides and parking garages can add up quickly to the equivalent of at least three kids on your gift list. It's about twenty minutes from the Triborough Bridge.

Denny's
254-45 Horace Harding Expressway, Little Neck
718-225-8833

A twenty-five minute drive on the Long Island Expressway (exit 32) can translate into lots of savings on children's clothing and layette items. With popular brands like Catimini, Mini Man, and Flapdoodle, you can feel great about buying designer fashions at a significant discount. They also have tons of outerwear, pajamas, hats, gloves, socks, and sweats. You'll quickly get over the fact that you didn't stroll down Madison Avenue or visit the chic shops downtown.

Stew Leonard's
100 Westport Avenue
Norwalk, Connecticut
203-847-7213

"Stew Leonard's had a little farm" is a song your children are sure to be chanting after a visit to this famous grocery store. An animal farm right out front, fresh ice cream, constant entertainment inside, wonderfully fresh baked goods, produce, meats, fish, coffee, and much more make this not-so-quick trip (just about fifty-five minutes) a must. In addition to the fresh goods, this store carries all of your household grocery needs. From paper goods and soaps to pasta, snacks, frozen foods, and cereals, you can fill up the over-sized carts and not go shopping again for a few weeks.

Wayne, New Jersey
Wayne Town Mall
Zany Brainy
201-890-7772

As the song goes, we're in love with this Jersey town! Price Club, Daffy's, Old Navy, Pizzeria Uno, and Zany Brainy all within two minutes of each other make this a perfect place to cross everything off your to do list. Zany Brainy, you ask? After you've told them "just two more minutes" while shopping in Price Club, Old Navy, and Daffy's, Zany Brainy is the place to make good on your bribes. Stop here for fun and educational toys, a quick read, and a spin around the Brio tracks. Pizzeria Uno is a great way to end the day—stuff their faces, load them back up in the car, and let them snooze on the thirty-five minute drive back to Manhattan.

Roosevelt Field Mall/Warehouse Mania
Garden City, Long Island
516-742-8000

Sometimes you really do need to go to a mall. And you'll be glad that you live about forty minutes from this one. Here you'll think you've just parked at the eighth wonder of the world. With all the top department stores you can ask for and more little stores than you can imagine, you can literally spend the entire day at this mall. What's more, the minute you leave the parking lot you can't miss Price Club, Home Expo (Home Depot's home design store), Toys 'R Us,

Kids 'R Us, Babies 'R Us ('R Us Serious?), Party City, Marshall's, T. J. Maxx, Sneaker Stadium. Oh, you're hungry? There's no need to worry with Nathan's, California Pizza Kitchen, Chili's, Burger King, Wendy's, McDonald's, and Bertucci's scattered about.

Current Events

All right, we'll admit it, twist our arms, some other publications and services exist that will help you stay on top of what's going on in this thriving metropolis and the surrounding environs. Here's a list of where you can look on a daily, weekly, or monthly basis for the latest and greatest:

On-line Services. If your three-year-old isn't hogging the family computer one hundred percent of the time, here are some new internet sites that provide interesting and timely information on events throughout the city. Just check out www.citysearch.com or www.sidewalk.com.

New York Magazine. The Cue section in the back has a listing of weekly events and other newsworthy stuff for children.

The New York Times. Friday Weekend Section includes a children's venue.

Time Out New York. The magazine has a kids section chock full of cool stuff to do. Don't we all want to be cool parents?

Local New York family publicaions are free and available in many outlets (e.g., bagel shops, pediatricians' offices, retail stores). Just remember to look in the corner by the door. These include *Big Apple Parents*, *New York Family*, and *Parent-Guide*.

New *Who Knews*

_____
_____
_____
_____
_____
_____
_____
_____
_____
_____
_____
_____
_____
_____
_____
_____
_____
_____
_____
_____
_____
_____
_____
_____

Try to keep a running tab of things you discover and would recommend for next year's edition. It'll help your life and, of course,
ours. If you have suggestions, you can send your e-mails to us at

whoknew@stmartins.com

or send us a letter at Who Knew Raising Kids in New York Could
Be This Easy?, c/o St. Martin's Press, 175 Fifth Avenue, New York,
NY 10010.

Index

clothing/shoe stores *(continued)*
  for specific items,
    90–91
  truly special, 86–88
concerts, 156, 157, 166–69
crafts, 56, 58, 73, 143, 161
cultural activities,
  145–59
  in Central Park, 145–50
  concerts, 156, 157,
  166–69
    at museums, 150–54
    in theaters, 154–59

D
dance classes, 48–50
Downtown book stores,
  126–28
drama classes, 58
drug stores, all-night, 32–33

E
electrolysis, 40
emergencies, 33
  CPR instruction, 7, 8,
  31–32
entertainers, 66–68

F
Faulhaber, Linda, 61
favors for parties, 70–71
fire houses, 153
fireworks, 169

G
gardens, 175, 176
Gramercy Park area, book stores in,
  124–25
gym classes, 45–48, 162

H
haircuts, 129–31

I
information, current, 181
Irish Echo, 7

K
kosher cakes, 69

L
last minute/temporary childcare, 18–19
libraries, 128

M
*Manhattan Directory of Private
  Nursery Schools* (Faulhaber), 61
Midtown toy stores, 119
mothers, support for, 34–40
museums, 150–54, 176
  outdoor concerts at, 167
  playgrounds near, 135–36
music classes, 52–56, 162, 163–64

R

resale stores, 27–28
restaurants, 94–113, 181
    child-friendly adult favorites,
    105–10
        family-friendly, 94–99
        for home-style food, 99–102
        for pizza, 110–13, 180
        for sweets, 102–5

S

safety for children, 29–33
    all-night pharmacies, 32–33
    babyproofing for, 29–31
schools:
    nursery, 60
    ongoing, 60
    see also preschools
shoe/clothing stores, 77–93, 179
    for bargains, 83–85
    for classics, 82–83
    for hip, hipper, hippest, 77–81
    one-stop, 88–90
    for shoes, 91–93
    for specific items, 90–91
    truly special, 86–88
shopping, *see* book stores; clothing/
    shoe stores; paraphernalia, stores
    for; resale stores; toy stores
shopping areas, playgrounds near,
    137–40
shopping trips, 179–81
skating, 171–72
sledding, 170–71
stores:
    bargain, 83–85
    drug, 32–33

for parphernalia, 23–27
    resale, 27–28
    see also book stores; clothing/
    shoe stores; drug stores; toy
    stores
strollers, 21–23
summer activities, 160–69
    at camps, 161–66
    outdoor, 166–69
summer au pairs, 11
support for parents, 34–40
    forums for, 37–39
    meetings for, 35–36
    for mothers, 34–35
    from professionals,
    36–37
surveillance services, 11–12
sweets, 102–5
swimming classes, 50–52

T

tax write-offs, 28
temporary/last minute childcare,
    18–19
theater for children, 154–59
Time Out New York, 181
toy stores, 114–21, 179, 180
    in Midtown, 119
    in TriBeCa/Village, 120–21
    on Upper East Side, 114–16
    on Upper West Side, 117–18
transportation of preschoolers,
    21–23
TriBeCa toy stores, 120–21
trips, quick, 174–81
    for fun, 174–78
    for shopping, 179–81